July 1, 2016

All love for our
wedding annivercry
on a special holiday

× ××

Ms. D'let

ECHOES OF BRITISH COLUMBIA

GW00459083

Robert Budd

foreword by SHERYL MacKAY

VOICES

from the

FRONTIER

ECHOES

OF

BRITISH

COLUMBIA

Harbour Publishing Co. Ltd.

PO Box 219

Madeira Park BC Canada V0N 2H0

www.harbourpublishing.com

Cataloguing data available from Library and Archives Canada

ISBN 978-1-55017-678-0 (paper)

ISBN 978-1-55017-630-3 (ebook)

Editing by Lucy Kenward

Cover design by Shed Simas

Cover photographs courtesy of Marian Hargrove (top left); BC Archives I-33187/Frank Cyril Swannell (top right); BC Archives A-02022 (bottom left); and Glenbow Archives NA-3439-3 (bottom right)

All photos courtesy of Royal BC Museum, BC Archives except where noted

CD compilation edited and produced by Robert Budd

CDs manufactured in China

Printed and bound in China

We gratefully acknowledge the financial support of the Canada Council for the Arts, the British Columbia Arts Council, the Province of British Columbia through the Book Publishing Tax Credit, and the Government of Canada through the Canada Book Fund for our publishing activities.

For Jessy, Levi, Emma and Mylie
and
Imbert and Ian, without whom these stories would be lost to time

Contents

Author's Note

ECHOES OF BRITISH COLUMBIA, the book and audio recordings, are intended to immerse you in the history of British Columbia: read the introduction to each story, listen to the speakers narrate their own experiences while you follow along in the text and look at the photos and the map. Discover a sense of place and meet the personalities who shaped the province, including interviewer Imbert Orchard, who occasionally speaks with and prompts his interviewees. Through these audio recordings, Orchard has provided a window into the remembered past, allowing British Columbians to speak for themselves.

I am hopeful that this book will provide a unique chance to experience the history of the province complete with a sense of the atmosphere of the times. Furthermore, I hope that these samples from Orchard's collection will encourage you to look for details about the aspects of BC's history that appeal to you, or look into details about your family history amid the material at the BC Archives or your local archive.

FACING: *The architect of all interviews in this book: between 1959 and 1966, oral historian Imbert Orchard and sound technician Ian Stephen travelled across the province collecting nearly a thousand interviews with British Columbia's old-timers. Photo courtesy of Nick Orchard*

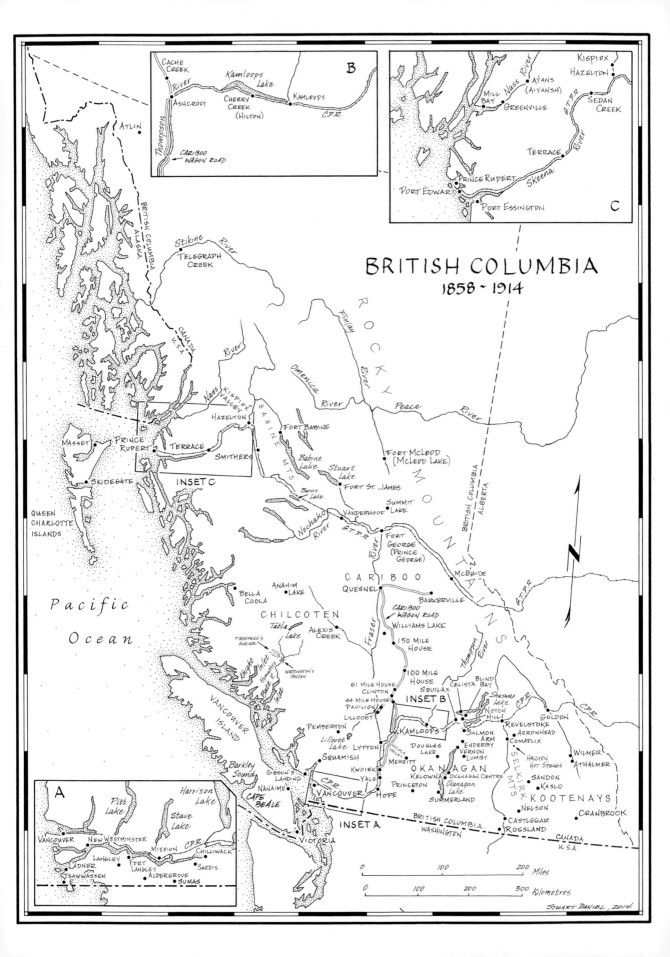

BRITISH COLUMBIA
1858 ~ 1914

Inset B:
CACHE CREEK · ASHCROFT · Thompson River · Kamloops Lake · CHERRY CREEK (HILTON) · KAMLOOPS · C.P.R. · CARIBOO WAGON ROAD

Inset C:
KISPIOX · HAZELTON · AYANS (AIYANSH) · Nass River · MILL BAY · GREENVILLE · G.T.P.R · SEDAN CREEK · TERRACE · Skeena River · PRINCE RUPERT · PORT EDWARD · PORT ESSINGTON

Inset A:
Pitt Lake · VANCOUVER · NEW WESTMINSTER · Stave Lake · Harrison Lake · LANGLEY · MISSION · CHILLIWACK · C.P.R. · FORT LANGLEY · SARDIS · LADNER · ALDERGROVE · TSAWWASSEN · SUMAS

ATLIN · Stikine River · TELEGRAPH CREEK · BRITISH COLUMBIA / ALASKA · CANADA / U.S.A. · ROCKY MOUNTAINS · Finlay River · Omineca River · Peace River · BRITISH COLUMBIA / ALBERTA

Nass River · Kispiox Valley · HAZELTON · BABINE MTS · FORT BABINE · Babine Lake · Stuart Lake · FORT McLEOD (McLEOD LAKE) · MASSET · PRINCE RUPERT · TERRACE · SMITHERS · INSET C · Burns Lake · FORT ST. JAMES · SKIDEGATE · Nechako River · VANDERHOOF · SUMMIT LAKE · G.T.P.R · QUEEN CHARLOTTE ISLANDS · FORT GEORGE (PRINCE GEORGE) · McBRIDE

Pacific Ocean · BELLA COOLA · ANAHIM LAKE · CARIBOO · QUESNEL · BARKERVILLE · CARIBOO WAGON ROAD · WILLIAMS LAKE · CHILCOTEN · Tatla Lake · ALEXIS CREEK · Fraser River · 150 MILE HOUSE · G.T.P.R · Tiedemann's Glacier · Waddington's Canyon · Knight Inlet · Homathko River · Bute Inlet · VANCOUVER ISLAND · Barkley Sound · 100 MILE HOUSE · CLINTON · 61 MILE HOUSE · 44 MILE HOUSE · PAVILION · LILLOOET · PEMBERTON · Lillooet Lake · CELISTA · BLIND BAY · SQUILAX · Shuswap Lake · C.P.R · NOTCH HILL · REVELSTOKE · GOLDEN · C.P.R · INSET B · KAMLOOPS · SALMON ARM · ARROWHEAD · COMAPLIX · LYTTON · DOUGLAS LAKE · ENDERBY · VERNON · LUMBY · WILMER · ATHALMER · GIBSON'S LANDING · SQUAMISH · NICOLA VALLEY · MERRITT · OKANAGAN · HALCYON HOT SPRINGS · SANDON · KASLO · KWOIEK · C.P.R · YALE · KELOWNA · OKANAGAN CENTRE · Okanagan Lake · SELKIRK MTS · CAPE BEALE · NANAIMO · VANCOUVER · HOPE · PRINCETON · SUMMERLAND · KOOTENAYS · NELSON · CRANBROOK · INSET A · BRITISH COLUMBIA / WASHINGTON · CASTLEGAR · ROSSLAND · CANADA / U.S.A. · VICTORIA · Thompson River

0 — 100 — 200 Miles
0 — 100 — 200 — 300 Kilometres

Stuart Daniel, 2014

It's in the Voice

SHERYL MacKAY
HOST/PRODUCER OF *NORTH BY NORTHWEST*, CBC RADIO BC

As soon as I opened my copy of *Voices of British Columbia*, I was hooked by hearing the stories of the province's pioneers written in the words of the people who had lived them. I arranged, via email, for author Robert Budd, or Lucky as he's known to friends, to come in for an interview about the book and the wonderful source material of the Orchard Collection at the BC Archives.

I am not sure who I was expecting to show up at the studio, but I do know that Lucky was a bit of a surprise. He looked younger than I imagined, and I soon realized he harbours the enthusiasm of about seven people! We talked about the book, he told some great stories, we played some audio from the collection, and by the end of the interview I knew I wanted him to be a regular part of *North by Northwest*. Happily, he thought that was a great idea too. But then you'd be hard-pressed to present Lucky with a project he wouldn't take on whole-heartedly.

That was four years ago, and since then Lucky has presented the stories of dozens of British Columbians in their own voices. Through his curatorial work with the Orchard Collection, he has connected people listening to the radio today with voices that link us to events and people of this place reaching back 150 years or more. I am so grateful that Lucky Budd is carrying on the work that Imbert Orchard and Ian Stephen started when they travelled this province fifty years ago.

There is something magical about listening to these voices with accents and pacing that we don't often hear on the radio. These folks are true storytellers, and I love how the little details in their stories really bring the history of BC to life: Minnie Caldwell discovering the benefits of being one of five girls in a frontier town filled with hundreds of men, Forin Campbell learning the hard way about how to drink whiskey when it's thirty below and Bob Gamman sleeping on the woodstove in order to survive his first winter as a greenhorn from England.

After one of Lucky's segments has played on *North by Northwest*, I often hear from listeners who have been touched by the stories in some way and want to add to them from their own family experiences, and sometimes I hear from descendants of the original speakers themselves.

How wonderful to open the pages of *Echoes of British Columbia* and find some of my favourite stories from the radio and learn more about these characters. I am sure you will enjoy meeting them too, as you take this special guided journey back through some very interesting pages of BC history.

Imbert Orchard's Time Machine

SOUND RECORDINGS are time machines, and oral histories in particular give us a personal connection to events and places often far removed from our own experience. It's this ability to learn about the past through the vivid stories of people who were there that has long drawn me to the study of history, and of British Columbia's oral history in particular.

In 2000, the Canadian Broadcasting Corporation was on a quest to have all of its audiotapes that were scattered across the various provincial archives digitized and catalogued. It was because of this initiative that I began working as an audio preservationist at the British Columbia Archives later that summer. Among the CBC material there are several important sound recordings, but the crown jewel, as far as I was concerned, was the Orchard Collection.

Sitting at my desk in the map mezzanine at the Archives, I would open up boxes of long-forgotten reel-to-reel tapes from that collection. With the crack of each case, I felt like Charlie Bucket opening one of Willie Wonka's chocolate bars to see if I had, in fact, exposed a golden ticket. Threading tape across the mechanisms of my tape player and into a take-up reel and hitting record on my CD burner, I would place the black padded headphones over my ears, close my eyes and be lost to history for the next thirty-two minutes.

Sure, I had to open my eyes from time to time to make notes. After all, my job included creating a finding aid so that users could easily locate material among the 2,090 tapes in the collection (998 interviews totalling 2,700 hours of material). Occasionally the tape broke down, and I would return to the twenty-first century to splice or bake or otherwise help the tape to play. And I often had to consult files to look up some pertinent information about when radio producer Imbert Orchard and sound technician Ian Stephen had recorded a particular interview. However, even as I stared out of the bright window at the tops of the trees dancing in the wind, the grey storm clouds gathering or the birds flying by, when the tape resumed I was always carried back to the 1960s.

Between 1959 and 1966, Orchard (1909–1991) and Stephen (1925–2012) travelled across British Columbia interviewing nearly a thousand of the province's old-timers. Their goal was to record "the story of the country"—what it was like to live and work and play in this wild and "unexplored" land—in the words of the people who had forged the first cities and industries and transportation networks. Today, these tapes constitute one of the largest oral history collections in the world. The Orchard Collection features such stellar sound quality that, to this day, it feels like you're in the room with the person being interviewed.

When I'm listening through the headphones, I'm first drawn in by the voice of a 72, 84 or even a 104-year-old telling me about events from before their time, or from their youth. However, the good interviewees, the true storytellers, through the nuance of their language, the pauses and breaths between their words, the intonation and emotion in their voice, immerse me in their world, at a specific time and place in our province's past. When I listened to Vera Basham describe her travels up the Nass River in the winter of 1915, I felt as if I was on that canoe with her. I could picture the piles of snow on the riverbank, the flow of the icy water, the build of the 18-year-old "Indian boy" who jumped into the frigid river to carry the passengers to shore. And I shivered alongside the woman huddled in her blanket and clutching the side of the vessel after falling overboard more than forty feet into the freezing river below. Now, of course, my imagination filled in many of the details, but the feeling of the journey, the facts of the story, have stuck with me and informed my impressions of the people and places of that time.

Sometimes, still, I find myself wondering: What would it have felt like to travel up the Nass River in November in a time before motorboats could power through? How would outsiders have been treated by the First Nations people guiding them along a waterway their ancestors had traversed for thousands of years? Would I have had the fortitude to endure such a journey in order to teach in a small, remote community, as Vera Basham did? And when I think about the stories in these terms—as a human being listening to the experiences of another human being, I can empathize with their struggles and their successes. These stories have much to teach all of us about what life was like around the turn of the twentieth century.

And what of the early days of such well-documented places as Barkerville? It is one thing to read in a history book that in the 1860s it was the largest settlement north of San Francisco, a thriving gold-mining town. But what was it like to be there? What were the people like? Unlike the history books that describe gold seekers or fortunes won and lost, Constance Cox tells us about Josephine, the woman who ran the dance hall and how she hated the cold winters. And through her story, we learn about the compassion and loyalty of those who lived in Barkerville, as Cox's uncle goes to great pains and expense to honour Josephine's dying wish of being buried in San Francisco. Beyond the facts of the story, I've come to appreciate how difficult travel was in those days, how remote Barkerville was and how cold it would have been in the winter. This story has made me think less about how much gold was found and more about the camaraderie of the people who lived there and the hardships they endured. How many women like Josephine, I wonder, travelled to this community to make a living but hated the harsh conditions in the north?

Although I finished digitizing the Orchard Collection some years ago, I have had the good fortune to continue working with the material. Throughout the course of my work at the archives, these stories became a passion of mine, leading first to a master's thesis about the collection, then to a book and eventually to a radio series on CBC's *North by Northwest*. That series, in which I play stories from the collection, has brought me into contact with people from all over the province who have been profoundly affected by these stories too. They tell me how much the anecdotes mean to them. They tell me how a place or a landmark mentioned in one of the interviews has more meaning now that they have a story attached to it. Occasionally they tell me that they have been reconnected with their own family history. One woman even emailed me to say she was driving along the highway listening to the radio and was stunned to hear the voice of her grandfather being interviewed. She pulled over to the side of the highway, tears streaming down her cheeks, as she pictured her grandfather, who had died more than forty-five years earlier. Like most listeners, she hadn't even known that the recording existed.

In 2010, I published a selection of stories from the collection in the book *Voices of British Columbia: Stories from Our Frontier*. The response to that book was incredibly positive, and since Orchard's collection covers a lot of geography and a wide range of subject matter, this second book adds to and expands upon the snapshot of the province provided in that first volume. My hope is that this collection continues to deepen our understanding of the people and events that shaped British Columbia and inspires a personal connection to the story of our province.

While it's important to know about the past, it's also essential to recognize that we, too, are shaping the place we live in. And our own stories—about our lives, our families, our struggles and our successes—are part of the fabric of the province. If you've been inspired by these stories, consider recording your own. In ten, forty, a hundred years, we will be the ancestors, and our stories—whether spoken or written or illustrated—will teach the next generation. The stories in this collection have much to instruct us: that our own daily lives are important and that the human voice can transcend time and place—if only we are open to listening.

So, as you read through the following pages, looking at the photos and listening to the accompanying CDs, allow these voices to carry you to another time and place. Immerse yourself in the wide-open landscapes, the wagon roads and the small-town streets. Imagine who you might meet along the way—an eager prospector, a reluctant homesteader or a happy-go-lucky remittance man. Like me, you may be captivated by these characters and imagine yourself right in the middle of the action.

FACING: *A group of locals lounging outside a saloon in Barkerville. Photo: c-09475*

(1)

An Urge to Go
to New Lands

IN 1857, New Caledonia—today, British Columbia—had a population of approximately 200 non-Native residents. However, when news of gold along the Fraser River reached prospectors in California a year later, a gold rush and the first wave of settlement began. Nearly 300,000 people had flocked to California in search of gold in 1849, but the area then entered a small depression and the gold seekers sought their fortunes farther north. By the spring of 1858, 30,000 immigrants had arrived.

Several other gold rushes followed, bringing more people and new infrastructure. Roads such as the Cariboo Wagon Road were built to connect the Lower Mainland with the gold fields in the Cariboo, and stopping houses and towns were established along the way. A railroad was laid to link British Columbia to eastern Canada, a trip that had previously taken months of travel by boat, and people from all over the world were able to access western Canada and its coal, metals, salmon

FACING: *The view from a CPR steamer as it arrives in Arrowhead, 1905. Photo: B-06650*

7

and timber. A global economic depression struck in the first decade of the twentieth century, but BC remained a land of possibility and its population swelled to more than 370,000 non-Native people by 1911.

The following stories relate the experiences of men and women who felt compelled to move west—or whose families did. Some came in search of adventure in a vast wilderness; others followed friends or family into established communities. Their recollections help us to understand the diverse realities of the province's early settlers.

What Did I Just Come Through?

ALBERT VERANOUS FRANKLIN

on Building a Road to the Gang Ranch

(RECORDED JULY 28, 1964)

THE CHILCOTIN First Nation were the first people to settle Tatla Lake. However, on March 15, 1892, Benjamin "Benny" Franklin purchased a ranch at Tatla Lake and he and his family, including his young son Albert (1884–1968), were among the first non-Native settlers in the Chilcotin region.

Benny Franklin set out to carve a route from the Chilcotin to Victoria via Knight Inlet. It took him and his guides six days to cross the 130 miles to the ocean, travelling by canoe, snowshoe, horse and on foot. The *Victoria Colonist* newspaper reported the following on April 13, 1892: "The two Indians who accompanied Franklin to Victoria had never been in a city before. Never seen a railway, a steamboat or a streetcar, and the Indians themselves were a curiosity to the city folks as well as they passed up Government Street with their bundles of furs on their backs and their rifles in hand." As the following anecdote further illustrates, Franklin was constantly trying to fashion new roads into Tatla Lake. He eventually sold his land to Robert Graham in 1902.

Today, Tatla Lake is a small unincorporated community located at the halfway point of Highway 20, which runs between Williams Lake to the east and the coastal community of Bella Coola to the west. For decades, however, Tatla Lake was known as the "end of the road" since it was the end of the Chilcotin Highway. In this case, the term "highway" really meant a poor horsetrack that wagon teams could bounce over.

ALBERT VERANOUS FRANKLIN: Maybe I should start from the time I was born.

IMBERT ORCHARD: Could we start even before that?

FRANKLIN: No, I wasn't here then. [laughs] I was born on Skykomish River in the year 1884 at two o'clock in the morning. My father was in— I was in the logging camp. Born in a logging camp. My father had an old log teamster, called— his name was John Gowan. And he was a splendid teamster. My father learned how to drive oxen through him. The Skykomish River emptied into the Snohomish River and they had agreed with the mill company that they'd put the logs in the Skykomish River on a certain date, and they had a shear boom to shear them off into a slough for the mill. Well, the day that everybody shot the logs, the shear boom was broken. And all the logs went past Everett, Washington, to the sea. And my father turned out broke. Nothing. He managed to pay all his help. When he got done, he had only 25 cents left. He decided to throw that away and start new. "But no," he says, "maybe the wife or kid might need something to eat," so he kept it.

And we moved up to Aldergrove. And my father started milking cows, making butter for Old Man York at Sumas. And he was doing pretty well, putting up good butter and milking cows—'course they were working hard—and in about four years' time, the surveyors was up around the Chilcotin Country surveying for the Grand Trunk Pacific Railroad, trying to bring it in by the way of Bute Inlet. 'Course there are pretty vicious mountains there. And they had Waddington's Canyon to tunnel through, also Tiedemann's Glacier to get around someway. It was a pretty difficult proposition. But, when they come back they had seen the Tatla Lake meadow. And the sidehills alongside of Tatla Lake, and they happened to stop in at York's place and they were talking to my dad, telling him what a wonderful

WATER ROUTE TO CHILCOTIN

Mr. Benjamin Franklin the Pioneer of a New Route for Cattle Imports.

Beef and Mutton for B. C. Markets— A Brace of Wondering Visitors.

"Benjamin Franklin, Chilcotin."

The name above quoted appears on the register at the Occidental, and the owner of the name is at present enjoying the comforts of civilization at the well known Wharf street hotel, having yesterday completed a not uneventful journey from his home in the wilderness, which may mean much for the great Chilcotin country.

Mr. Franklin went in by way of Ashcroft, some time ago, attracted by the manifold advantages the Chilcotin plains present to the cattle rancher. The necessity of opening up these plains by placing them in communication with the markets of the cities of British Columbia, quickly presented itself to him, and his trip down was very much of an experiment—an experiment destined to prove the feasibility of direct communication with Chilcotin via Knight's Inlet and the water route to Victoria.

Tatla lake was left behind on March 16th, and travelling by horse and on foot, by snowshoe and by canoe, Mr. Franklin reached Knight's Inlet, accompanied by his two Chilcotin Indian guides, in six days— the distance traversed being a little over 130 miles of unknown country. The route taken developed few obstacles, and Mr. Franklin hopes to induce the early construction of a road, which will benefit amazingly the now thinly settled, but promising country. A shorter route to the Chilcotin, or a more feasible, he does not think could be found.

All the land back of Knight's Inlet and between it and Tatla Lake abounds in the most nourishing grasses, and there is no reason why it should not supply the markets of British Columbia with prime beef and mutton. Close to the inlet hops are now raised, though, of course, in small quantity, and all kinds of vegetables thrive and flourish. With a little dyking this section of the country would be made even more fertile than the famed Fraser valley.

The two Indians who came down with Mr. Franklin have never been in a city before, never saw a railway train, a steamboat or a street car, and were as much a curiosity to pedestrians as they passed up Government street, last evening, with their bundles of furs on their backs and their rifles in hand, as those pedestrians were to them.

Benny Franklin's new route from the Chilcotin makes headlines in the Daily Colonist. *Scan courtesy of the* Times Colonist

The Chilcotin Valley near Alexis Creek, ca. 1925. Photo: A-01581

meadow that was. There was even sugarcane growing there and there was bunch grass on the sidehill the full length of Tatla Lake, up to the horse's knees. What a wonderful place to raise cattle. So my father sold out his butter making and milking business and moved up there. He had something like $4,000 saved up.

We moved up there, and he had a wagon and he got a team of horses, and he come up by the old road alongside of the Fraser River, and stopped in at Ashcroft and got some groceries and stuff and went on up and we had to swim the horses at Soda Creek to get over into the Chilcotin Country because we was headed for Tatla Lake. He knowed about it on account of these surveyors telling him all about it. And they had surveyed right through the flat where we built our home. So, anyway, he come on up and when he got as far as Alexis Creek, there was no more road. So we had to make the roads from Alexis Creek through bull pastures—there's bull pastures alongside of the river there— Chilcotin River, you know, we're not on the Fraser River anymore, and an Indian come along and says, "You want some *mawich*?" "*Maika tiki mawich*?" he said. That's Chinook, now.

ORCHARD: What's it mean?

FRANKLIN: "Do you want some deer meat?" My father says, "*Nawitke*." He could talk Chinook, too.

Pack horses swimming across the Chilcotin River, 1904.
Photo: I-58390/Frank Cyril Swannell

So away he went, trotting on ahead. And all he had was a knife about, oh, ten inches long overall, handle and everything. And that's all he had to get that deer with. He, he was just before we got to Redstone Flat we caught up to him. Here he had a deer, sure enough, wasn't a big one. He'd creeped up onto it on his hands and knees so that it wouldn't hear him, and he stabbed it while it was laying down. And he had it all dressed and ready for us when we arrived there. We all had *mawich* to eat, that's deer. We had plenty. And when we got to Tatla Lake, Old Gishawn, the fellow that killed the deer, he claimed that he was the owner of the Tatla Lake place because no king or queen ever come to see him to ask him for it, so it was his. Well, that was all right. My father bought it from him for a caddy of T&B tobacco. That was the price he paid for the Tatla Lake place. Well, we established a home there. My father got some groceries and dry goods and so forth from Ashcroft, had to go to Ashcroft to get them, and he started a store with the Indian selling the goods: calico and stuff to make the dresses out of, and Jew's harps, they liked to play them. And, when we had to go for supplies we had to go clear to Ashcroft.

After we got all settled and started to accumulate a little from selling our goods, my father had to go to Ashcroft to get some goods and he found out that there was a ferry boat at the Gang Ranch. So he made the road, I was with him, and he had Gilpin as a guide, an Indian, to guide him to make the road from the Chilcotin Bridge through to the Gang Ranch. And when he got there, he got off, tied up his horse and went over to talk to [James] Prentice that lived in a big mansion there. Told Prentice that we had a road through from Chilcotin Bridge to the home ranch. "No, Franklin, you're a darned liar," he says, "there's no road there." "What did I just come through? I just made it. Just got done." And he spent about $150 to pay for the Indian and the food and so forth, the cost, for to get that road through because he was going to Ashcroft to get his supplies.

And, when we got across the ferry, we come on down, up Dog Creek, it's—you're going upstream there, and come out at the 61 Mile House, and then on down to Clinton. When he got to Clinton, he stopped and a fellow walked out in the street, "Your name Mr. Franklin?" My father said, "Yes, sir, and I'm proud of it." "Well," he says, "I'm the tax collector," and he says, "I'm going to collect toll taxes from you for the use of the road." And my father just got done paying $150 to build the road. "Well," my father says, "I'm not going to pay it." "Well," he says, "Well, I'm going to take your rig, your horses and wagon." He says, "You'll take them over my dead body!" Well, he never did pay it. That was $150 toll tax that he never paid. Do you blame him? I don't.

Located at the end of the Chilcotin Highway, Tatla Lake marked "the end of the road" in the 1890s. Photo: 1-57385/Frank Cyril Swannell

Just Try and Throw Us Off

FLORENCE REEDMAN

on Homesteading in the Shuswap

(RECORDED MAY 14, 1965)

JOHN REEDMAN (1856–1930) was born into an upper-class British family and ran the family furniture business. He was also an auction-eer and government representative in charge of levying certain taxes. John had been widowed twice, and Florence Harriet Cave (1881–1968) of Stamford, England, was his housekeeper and the caretaker of his three children until the two married in 1902. She was twenty-six years younger than him. The couple had eight more children, though one died in infancy and another at age 15.

The family felt compelled to leave England when a good friend of John's committed suicide after his gambling debts were uncovered, and because many of John's class-conscious friends made hurtful comments toward Florence. The family travelled to Canada in 1905 aboard the steamship *Virginian* and then moved west to Calgary, where they met with John's son Harry. The family was looking to make a fresh start, which included a new vocation for John.

In the following story, Florence Reedman describes how the family established themselves by homesteading in Blind Bay, at the south end of Shuswap Lake, in the first decade of the 1900s. This story conveys a sense of isolation and teamwork as well as gender roles, and it paints a picture of how much work was involved in acquiring things like flour that we now take for granted.

·   ·   ·

FLORENCE REEDMAN: At that time, in England, all over the British Isles, you saw big placards. CPR, of course, were boosting this country, because they got the railway through. "Go to Canada. Go to British Columbia—the land of milk and honey." And there was pictures of apple trees, and the apple trees were big silver dollars. Very enticing, you know. And that was why we came.

So rather than give up all this interest, because he was very comfortably fixed, he sent his eldest son. And so Harry came out, and he eventually got to Edmonton. Well, he was musical, he played the piano very nicely, and he got in with nice people, was having a good time, he got work, and everything was lovely. Wrote to see, so of course, my husband set the wheels going to dispose of all his businesses and come out. And we left England the sixth of April, got across the ocean, we got in to Newfoundland, we saw the beautiful icebergs, and we had to go 300 miles out of our course. We were admiring these beautiful, oh, you know, just like diamonds shining in the sunlight. We were nine days crossing, and he told us that we didn't realize how close to death we were with these icebergs, see? Then we came back. Then we got to Calgary, and Harry was there to meet us. He'd come down from Edmonton, and we were staying in a hotel.

There were nine of us in our party. One or two gentleman farmers coming to look at land, and one of them, Sunday morning, went to church. And he came home and he says, "Jack," he says, "I've just met a man from Uffington," and that was two miles out of my husband's city of— town of Stamford, "and he said he would like to meet you." This man, and his son, they were coming to British Columbia. It seemed his son, the year before, had gone to British Columbia, had heard so much about it, you know, and growing fruit and that,

Blind Bay, on Shuswap Lake, 1930s, was the property of the Columbia River Logging Company when the Reedman family arrived. Photo: C-06926

and he got off at Salmon Arm. Of course, you see the Shuswap Lake at Salmon Arm. They wandered along the logging trails, and eventually they struck Blind Bay, and they thought it was such a beautiful spot, that's where they wanted to go. So he went back to Calgary, and told my husband about this beautiful lake. So Dad says, "Well, we were going to Lloydminster, in the Barr Colony," and he says, "Man, you can't take a young wife there, you'll kill her." [laughs]

So, we decided we'd throw our lot in, and we came to— came to British Columbia. And we got landed at Notch Hill and saw that the grass was knee deep, my husband says, "This'll do." But he didn't realize, when we got down onto the lake, it was nothing. Just as I had told you: the mountains and the lake and the forest. There wasn't a living soul. And to get supplies, oh, we brought to a quantity of— a big tent and one of these awful old tin stoves, and different things that we needed, to start. And we camped out. And we were under canvas for twenty-six weeks.

They blazed a trail from Blind Bay to Notch Hill. It's a 900-foot rise and down again. Once a week, they left camp and left myself and my companion, a friend from England. I said, "I'm not going to be the only woman." There was— the others were all men, you see, except my husband, his three sons and these other gentlemen, and myself and my 2-year-old son born in England. And I want a companion. So this girl had lost her parents and she was at a loose end. My husband says, "Well, I'll finance you if you'll come with us." So she came. She's still in Canada. And they would leave Saturday morning and go, seven o'clock, and we wouldn't have a particle of food in camp until they'd come back at seven o'clock at night. There was nothing, the camp was stripped. They ate like wolves, you know. They were working out and starting to clear land. And they were so hungry. And I'll tell you how we got a roast of meat once a week. This is a good one. [laughs]

Archie, the middle boy, lived on the point. He would— they would go up to Notch Hill and he'd walk the track. That was twenty-one miles from Notch Hill to Salmon Arm. And towards evening, buy a piece of meat, roast the meat and pack it. Then get on the train, and then he'd have to walk from Notch Hill down to our camp to the lake. He'd get home at two o'clock Sunday morning. That's how we got a piece of meat once a week. There was nothing there, you know. A little store in Notch Hill. There was a post office.

One time I sent the list up and I wanted cheese, all commodities. There was cheese and bacon and flour, big items. And then Dad came back, he says, "Well, Mother, I don't know what we're going to do for next week." There wasn't— the— Old McIntyre didn't have any flour, he didn't have any cheese and he didn't have any bacon. He got a few of the other things. So what my husband responded to, they wrote to Enderby flour mills—Murphy's flour mills, they were in those days—and ordered a half a ton of flour. They came to Notch Hill on the train, of course. Well then, to get it down to Blind Bay, the only man that had a team of horses was this old storekeeper. And we had to get him to bring it. And he had to take it right round from Notch Hill to Balmoral, and then down a logging trail to the end of the bay. And that's how we got in through that. And when we got to the end of the day, we had nine huge packing cases.

The Columbia River Logging Company, ca. 1908. They threatened to throw the Reedmans off their cleared land. Photo: D-03623

The Railway Station at Notch Hill, 1930s. Photo: B-05603

And then all our blankets and pillow-bedding and that. And Dad and the boys had to chop down trees and make a raft, which they tied together with rope, and put our goods and chattels in this. And we towed down to the spot they'd chosen to live. Talk about Robinson Crusoe. [laughs]

We homesteaded, but we were there for many years. And they wouldn't— they wouldn't give us anything. They said we were on timber limit and they couldn't give us the land. It belonged to the Columbia River Lumber Company. So one of the land inspectors came one day and he was telling my husband this. And he said, "Well," he says, "just try and throw us off." He says, "We've been here five years now." At that time, of course, we had a house. All this lumber had to come from Kualt Mill. It had to come by steamboat, because there were no way of getting it. And it was ordered in May and it wasn't delivered till August. They had the basement dug, and they had to get it up. And on the 15th day of October, we moved in. We had a rowboat by that time. The boys had built a boat. And they brought all our stuff in rowboat to the house. So all this happened, as I just related, 1905.

Yes, we only had squatter's rights. They told us that. And we were there for ten years before we got deeds. By that time, we had land cleared and fruit trees in. We were taking an awful risk. But, you see,

Reedman's store in Blind Bay, as it stood in the 1930s.

Photo: C-06919

the Columbia River Company weren't doing anything. They'd taken on— My husband says, "You're quite welcome to all the logs you'll find on this piece of property." There were none there. They'd cut it all down. And up where we had our orchard, it was benchland. They'd had a big fire the year before, and it just ruined all the stand— the timber there. Of course, there was beautiful trees, beautiful fir trees and cedars. And do you know how they cleared it? Dug round the roots and tapped them, felled the trees, sawed them up by hand and burnt them. And Dad would say, "Oh, what they'd give for this wood in England."

IMBERT ORCHARD: How did they know how to do this? Did they have the tools—

REEDMAN: They didn't know. My husband was a businessman. As he said, the heaviest thing he ever lifted was a pencil, or a pen. Just had the— Isn't it funny English people get that urge to go to new lands. And he was stricken with a form of rheumatism. For three months, he couldn't feed himself. He couldn't dress himself. And one morning, I had him laying there in the tent. And I used to— Our doctor was very good. He gave us— me a wonderful first aid kit. I had everything in it, even sutures and everything. And he says, "Oh, you can do it if you have to." And this morning, a little steamer came tooting along. And I said, "Oh, who's coming?" Of course, great excitement, all the rest down. And "How many men have you got here?" "So-and-so." "Well, we want them all. There's a big fire up at Celista Creek." "That's not Celista. The creek's way up." And some valley with timber was on fire. It was just struck by lightning and as it is and, "We want men." Well, the boys were gone for nine weeks. It was a terrific fire. And here was myself and my companion and a 2-year-old boy, and a 14-year-old boy, the youngest of the three stepsons. They didn't take him. And my husband laying there helpless. And my companion and the 14-year-old boy walked the blaze trail every Saturday morning to go and pack the groceries down. What a time. [laughs]

Money? I should say! Luckily my husband was comfortably off. You see, he planted the orchard, twelve acres of it, now clear cut twelve acres of land, and had to hire this old Scotchman's storekeeper's team of horses from Notch Hill to do that work, you see, because we couldn't have cows or a team until— anything until we got land cleared. There wasn't any- where where they— it was all timber forests, you see. You couldn't— it wasn't as though, like on the prairies, turn them out to feed.

Well, then the night we landed in the house, my husband sent to Van- couver and bought some furniture—bought some beds and bedsteads, of course. So we all went to bed. Oh, we got to have a lovely night's sleep. We got to sleep in real beds. All this twenty-six weeks, we'd slept on cedar- bough beds on the tent floor, you know. Every week, they were all— the youngest son had to go out and cut fresh cedar boughs. And you laced them, you know. And it smells beautiful the first night. And it's very soothing. But at the end of the week, they begin to get rather lumpy. [laughs] So we thought we'd visualize a lovely night's sleep, real beds. Next morning, one came down. "How did you sleep?" "Rotten." Next one, "How did you sleep?" "Rotten." The third one came, "Well, and how did you sleep?" "I'm going to sleep on the bed floor tonight." [laughs] Oh dear.

Then in 1907, people started settling over Celista. Well, those people had to row over in their boats to our— to Blind Bay, and then walk our trail or the lakeshore to Sorrento that is now, in our days was Trapper's Landing, and then walk the pony trail to Notch Hill. Well, often they'd come over, and they go up and come back very weary, and I'd give them some tea, and they couldn't start home because the lake was rough. Couldn't go, they'd have to stay all night.

And eventually they worried my husband to build a store. He said, "Dash it all, I left England to get away from business. I want to forget business." However, they kept up—even the Indians offered him land at Squilax. There's a store at Squilax now—to build a store there, so they'd have a store at Squilax. You see, there was nothing there then. And, no, he didn't like the idea of— they'd give him a ninety-nine-year lease, you see, but he didn't quite like that idea, so he built one at Blind Bay. And after 1912, he used to carry the mail for each person, and stop at their houses, and bring the mail for the Celista people, and they'd get it when they'd come over. So then eventually, the government appointed him postmaster, 1912. He died in 1930, October, and I carried on until 1943, when I collapsed with a heart condition.

Sixth of January, 1912, and they went over as usual on Friday to take supplies to the settlers at Celista. And of course it was an all-day business. Coming home, they were arriving home about six o'clock in this terrible storm. And they couldn't make the shore because of the ice that had flown up from Sorrento. Eventually, they drifted into the middle of the bay, of Blind Bay. And before morning, it was the most beautiful moonlit night and it was twenty-seven below zero. And our motor launch was frozen solid in the ice. And they had no heat and no food. And they were there all night. There were about five of them—five or six of them: a little Scots girl, Brown from Celista that was helping me at the time. And I stood on that shore nearly all night, twenty-seven below zero, wrapped up, watching that boat freeze in there in the ice. 'Cause the moon was shining down on it, so you could see all the movements.

So the next morning, my husband said, "Well." He says, "We can't stay and freeze to death. Who's going to try the ice?" Nobody volunteered but himself. And he was the oldest, you see. So he took the pike pole and he says, "Well, boys, follow me. If I don't go through, you follow me." He took the pike pole and felt it. And he got safely to shore. And then they came along. And I knew the boat was there. And they'd been to sea. And we got the field glasses out, the boys did. "Well, Mother, they're coming." So we got a roaring fire going. And they came home. They were pretty cold, of course. They had the hot breakfast. And then they went into the warm sitting room and they dropped like flies, went to sleep.

ORCHARD: They hadn't been able to sleep all night.

REEDMAN: Oh no, no. I thank God that night.

The Last of the Old Western Days

GUY LAWRENCE

on Travelling to the Klondike

(RECORDED IN 1972)

HISTORY BOOKS are often filled with success stories. However, oral histories also provide us with tales of failure. This gold rush story from Guy Lawrence was one of tens of thousands where the goal was not achieved.

Gold was discovered in the Yukon in August of 1896. When the news broke the following year, a stampede of over 100,000 would-be-prospectors tried to get to the gold fields in the Klondike, during a rush that lasted from 1897 to 1899. There was no doubt that travel and living conditions were harsh, and the journey proved so arduous that only 35,000 arrived. Guy Lawrence (b. 1880) is one of those who failed to make it.

In this anecdote recorded when he was 92 years old, he details the circumstances under which he and his father, John Cousins Lawrence, left England in February 1898 to try their luck in the gold fields. John Lawrence was a man of means. A silver medallist at the Royal Academy, he had painted portraits of such high-profile people as the Duke of Cambridge, and later after his return from Canada, a posthumous portrait of the World War I French flying ace Georges Guynemer for the French government. However, at the turn of the century, he had embarked on a much different adventure.

The 17-year-old Guy Lawrence was forced to end a relationship in order to travel to Canada with his father, and the slow drawl of his voice perfectly captures their long drawn-out journey to the Klondike,

an experience fraught with setbacks and long periods of waiting for help. Had they actually made it to the Yukon, the Lawrences would have had a much more arduous journey, as gold seekers had to cross either the Chilkoot or White Pass trails to the Yukon River, and the law stated that they had to carry a year's supply of food to prevent starvation. In all, those supplies weighed close to a ton. When there were no animals to transport the heavy, cumbersome goods, they were often hauled using a hand-sleigh, a wood and metal sleigh with a twine rope at the front that was pulled by hand.

In the end, the Lawrences made it to Atlin, sixty kilometres south of the Yukon border. Five thousand miners flocked to the area in 1899, making the Atlin gold rush among the richest offshoots of the Klondike gold rush. Today the community is home to the Taku River Tlingit First Nation in whose language Atlin means "big body of water." Gold is still found in the area, and it is estimated that $23 million in gold has been extracted since the first discovery.

.   .   .

GUY LAWRENCE: When my father told me that he wanted me to come with him to Canada, I was quite surprised. And really I wasn't very pleased. I had a love affair on with a young lady who had been to school with my sister.

CD1, TRACK 3

I only had three days' notice to say goodbye to my friend. And then we sailed from Liverpool over to Halifax. And crossing the continent, we had quite a few experiences, which are usual on CPR in wintertime. And we stayed off three days at different places. If my father had listened carefully to a conductor on the train on the western division, he need never have gone to the Klondike. This conductor was walking up and down the aisles of the different compartments, trying to sell 2,000 shares of Crowsnest Coal for $2 a share. In three years, they rocketed to $78. And my father had plenty of money, which he was carrying in a belt.

We tried to outfit in Vancouver. But the rush of stampeders had cleared all the stores out. So we went over to Victoria. And we finally outfitted there. All passenger steamers had long ago been used to a great extent from all over the civilized world to go to this gold rush. At least

FACING: *Guy Lawrence and his father left England to try their luck in the Klondike gold fields, but only made it as far as Atlin, BC. Photo:* E-02855

90,000 people went up there in two years. We boarded a China tea-trade boat, which had been taken off her usual run, and had something like eight or ten or twelve cabins. And there were 600 of us on board. Two hundred of the passengers were militia going up to assist the North-West Mounted Police keep order in the north. We made a straight run to Wrangell, Alaska. When we got to Wrangell, we saw the last of the old Western days. Guns were popping all the time, but I can't say that I saw anybody shot. I think most of the shooting was exuberance.

Unfortunately for us, just about that time had passed a law that nobody could enter the North with less than a year's provisions. And between the provisions and the hardware we took with us, we had at least two tons of stuff. We left Wrangell and went to the mouth of the Stikine River. And the Stikine River was still covered with ice, except right at the very mouth. We were forced to stay on the island four weeks. During that time, I did lots of sailing with the boat. And my father, he spent his time bathing in the water amongst the icebergs that were breaking off. We tied our boat out when the river opened. And we found that we couldn't possibly make it to Telegraph Creek, 160 miles. We tried the boat empty. And I think we sailed for five or six miles upstream with a spanking wind behind us. And then we went on the bend of the river, and we lost the breeze and had to row. We couldn't make headway with the empty boat. So we gave up the idea, and went back to the island again and decided to wait for a steamer to pick us up.

There were numerous steamers due as soon as the ice went out of the river. The first steamer that went up the river was very aptly named the *Monte Cristo*. It was a small sternwheeler, and they carried no passengers but thirty tons of hard liquor for the miners in

Ice on the Stikine River delayed Lawrence's venture upriver by four weeks. Photo: I-21808/BC Government

the Interior. At last we were able to flag a larger steamer down, and the captain took us aboard. This boat had evidently been taken out of mothballs. She had very little power. She went up the river all right until we got to the Grand Canyon. Every river in the north seems to have a Grand Canyon, and the Stikine River was no exception. We got to the canyon, took on wood, which some of the stampeders had cut during their stay there, and then the next morning the boat puffed and snorted out to the canyon. It couldn't make any speed at all and finally we were drifting back. The captain was very excited. He left the wheelhouse, went down to the engine department, took a monkey wrench and screwed the valve down. And this time we made a little better speed until we came to a point sticking out in the river and we could not get by that point. Anyway, just at that moment somebody shouted, "man overboard!" And it appeared that the engineer preferred to risk drowning than being blown up by his boiler. We were nine days tied up at the canyon when a much more powerful and later-built boat named *Stikine Chief* took us off and we went up to within twelve miles of Telegraph Creek. We spent about five weeks on the winter trail and we only made thirty-six miles ahead, we had to relay so much with our two tons of stuff. And then we denned up for the winter.

When February came, we hit the trail again but we had discarded a lot of our hardware and quite a lot of our food. In the meanwhile, a new mining camp had been found, and that was Atlin on the very border of Yukon, but still in BC—about forty miles from the boundary. And we decided, or rather my father decided, that we'd go to Atlin instead of going down to the Yukon. Well, it's a long story about getting over that trail. We had quite a few experiences which weren't very pleasant. When we got to Atlin a law had just been passed that no alien could hold a claim. This was disastrous for the simple reason that all those men had been hand-sleighing like we had—we were fourteen months—and they'd been doing the same thing. The consequence was that all their claims were seized by British subjects. Some of them were staked four and five times.

My father's first experience with mining was he bought a bench claim very close to Fritz Miller's claim. And Fritz Miller was the discoverer of

Fritz Miller's discovery claim in Atlin, 1900. Photo: B-04120

Atlin. It was a bench claim, and it looked very promising. And we looked into this red gravel. And we saw three nuggets. They were mighty small, but they were nuggets. Gold was worth $16.50 an ounce then. My father carefully removed the nuggets, wrapped them up in tissue paper and mailed them home. Several weeks later, we got the letter from home, from my mother and sister, saying what clever miners we were. That was the total amount of gold on that claim. It was a bare claim. And they had simply salted it with those three nuggets.

Show Me a Good Ranch

MARY BAKER

on Settling in the Nicola Valley

(RECORDED OCTOBER 28, 1965)

CLAUDE PAUL "Henry" Steffens, a Swiss man born in Germany, was an officer in the German navy for sixteen years. He married Sofia Steffens in England. The couple had two children there before they moved to British Columbia in 1885, where Henry got a job working for the CPR in Ashcroft. When construction continued west, he and his growing family, including daughter Mary (b. 1889), moved to Lytton where he bought a hotel that he turned into a store. He also started to drive cattle to Lillooet.

The Thompson and Thompson River Salish First Nations have inhabited the area around Lytton for 10,000 years. By the time the Steffenses arrived in the 1880s, Lytton was already a very established place. For many years, it had been a major stop on transportation routes, namely the River Trail from 1858, the Cariboo Wagon Road in 1862 and was in the process of becoming part of the Canadian Pacific Railway in the 1890s. After ten years living in Lytton, Henry Steffens decided to become a rancher and farmer so he took up a pre-emption in the Nicola Valley and moved his wife and seven children there. After staking claim to his 160 acres of land, he was required to spend three years "improving upon it" before the government would give him the land. Unfortunately, however, he died just a few years after the family had moved and established their home. Although she was advised to move to Merritt to raise the children, Sofia stayed on the pre-empted land, which was fourteen miles from town, and together she and her boys built a quality farm and cattle ranch.

Mary Baker represents the first generation of children born to settlers in the British Columbia countryside, and her narrative reveals several important character traits tied to her upbringing. These include her leadership as the "boy" in her family because she was older than her male siblings, and her strength and independence. She also shares many details about her father and her childhood in the Nicola Valley. In 1907 at 100 Mile House, she married Fred Baker, an immigrant from England who ran a freighting business, and she discusses her life as a wife and mother living on farms in the Nicola Valley. Throughout she mentions the helpful attitude of the "Indians," without whom many settlers would have suffered or perished.

. . .

CD1, TRACK 4 MARY BAKER: I was born in a little place called Kwoiek. My dad used to work out there when he first came here. Then before he moved into Lytton and bought the store. And I was born there and I was quite a small child and they moved into Lytton and they lived in there and they bought the store and he lived there, I guess, till I was about 10 years old.

Well, when I was in Lytton, it was a very small little town, and I had an uncle that lived in the halfway house. And my mother used to let me go up there for my holidays. And they had a stage from Lytton to Lillooet. And when I was very small, I couldn't have been anymore than about eight, and I remember going up on the stage and we went, we only went about four miles from my uncle's and then we all had to get out and walk to my uncle's. The Lillooet road never went any further. They were just building it. So they used to put the mail and the express and everything like that on the horses, and the passengers walked, walked as far as my uncle's. He kept the kind of— a licenced house and a hotel. And then he'd stay there overnight and then he'd ride the horse and pack everything into Lillooet by horseback. And he kept up all the passengers that came. They stayed there at night, it was a regular hotel, then my aunt gave meals and my uncle sold liquor and he also had a farm. And he kept everyone from, you know, coming and going, from all over the country

A stagecoach on the Cariboo Wagon Road, 1900s. Photo: A-09777

which, you know, prospectors and one thing another. And it was, it was quite a lively place, you know.

His name was Charlie McGillivray. Yes, he was a very fine man. And the house was burnt down, they had a lot of people come there that day. My aunt was quite busy and the little girl, she went into the bedroom and she set fire to the house. And there was a chap working not very far from the house and he happened to look up and see the smoke, you know? So, he came running over to my uncle and he says, "The house is afire, don't you know the house is afire?" Uncle says, "No, where's the fire?" Well, he says, "Well, just look, go out the back. The smoke is rolling out, the whole place afire!" So he rushed in there, it was in a back room, and the little girl was sitting on the bed and the whole room was afire. And this man, he jumped through the window and grabbed the little girl and went right through the flames and took her out. Oh, she was badly burned, but 'course the place burnt down. And then he rebuilt it after that. And oh, everybody was so good to them. The Indians hauled lumber for him and, oh my, they were nice. But he was a very fortunate man, you know, because everyone was so kind.

So there was a lot of ranches, but those people that came in there, what they were, were squatters. And as years went by, when other people came in and went to the government office, they found out that this land was— really had never been taken up. Others tried to take it away from them, but they had the right, you see, because they were there first. I think there was a squatter's right. And I think they really recorded it and really claimed it afterwards.

An inn on the Lillooet road. Photo: G-00793/Charles Gentile

And then after that, my dad decided that he'd like to go farming. And so he sold his store and went up to the Nicola Valley. Well, in fact, an Indian came along one day, and my dad said to him there, "Do you know where there's any good ranches in the Nicola Country?" And he said, "Oh yes," he said, "I know where there's a good place." So he said, "Well, I'll tell you," he said, "I'll give you $50," he said, "if you'll take me up to the Nicola Valley and show me a good ranch." And then the Indian—of course that was a lot of money to an Indian in those days—so he said, "Yes." So my dad got a couple of pack horses—my oldest brother was home from college at the time, he was going to college in New Westminister—so he took my brother and the Indian and he took them up to the ranch where they are today. And it turned out to be a very fine place.

Henry Steffens, ca. 1870, died shortly after moving his family to the Nicola Valley, leaving his wife and children to adapt to the ranching life on their own. Photo: G-07776

So, but some of my brothers was born there, so we moved up there. And oh, we had to go by, we had to load everything up in the wagons, you know, and drive up there with regular, with just regular, well you might say, immigrants. [laughs] Because everything had to go by team. There was nowhere— there was no train at that time. The trains hadn't came through to Nicola. So we went up by the wagon and located on the— on this new pre-emption. 'Course it took a lot of hard work and my dad built a cabin there and then, there, several of my brothers was born up there. In fact, there was about four. A big family of boys. We're seven, eight, eight boys. So, there was a lot of children.

And there was a lot of hard work. But course, I did the, I was the boy, because I was older really, older than the other children. Of course, I had to do the boys', take the boys' parts mostly, till I was old enough, you know, to— the other boys to help me. And, then when I went up the Cariboo Road; I had an aunt up there and she wanted somebody to come up and stay with her, so my mother sent me up to my aunt up on the Cariboo Road. I was about 16. No, about 15 at the time. Well, it was quite adventure to me, for me too, you know?

And we went up on stagecoach. We left in the morning, about four

83 Mile House, one of Mary Baker's stops on the way to visit her aunt, ca. 1920. Photo: A-03894

o'clock, and then we went up to Hat Creek and had breakfast, then into Clinton and on up the road. We stopped at the 83 that night and then on up to the 44, where my aunt was. So, I stayed there with her. And, oh my goodness, it was quite adventure for me, you know. It was so different and, 'course, it was my uncle up there, he had a big cattle ranch. He run about 1,500 head of cattle. So I stayed there for about three years, and during that time I was there, I got married. Then I came on back, and I lived in Ashcroft for about eight years and then my husband took this place up here. And, 'course, he didn't do a thing to it for several years and then he finally had to improve on it, you know, and live here. So he said, "Well, Mother," he said, "I guess we'll have to go on the ranch." I said, "Oh, my goodness, do we have to go up there?" [laughs] And it looked terrible grim to me. So we came on up and there was no— it had— he'd got a chap to come and build a little cabin for him, and in the meantime, he'd got a load of freight to go to Barkerville. So he said, "Anyway," he said, "I'll have to go up to the ranch, you know, I can't lose the ranch now." He said, "I done quite a lot of improvements on it and somebody's got to stay on it." Well, I said, "All right, then," I said, "I'll go up." And, when he was leaving that morning he said, "Well, Mother, here's the team of horses and there's their harness." And he'd built a corral and hung the harness on the fence, you might say, and he said there, "Well, do the best you can till I get back." Which was about six weeks. [laughs] Seemed a long, grim time, didn't it?

And I had two children then, one was 2 and the other was 4, so I said, "Oh yes, I'll be all right here as long as I have a horse to—." One of the horses I could ride, then I had a little buckboard that I could drive if I wanted to go. And then I had to go across the river and out up the road, you know, along there, over the, up the hills and pretty miserable to go. But anyway, I stayed here until he came back and did all kinds of things, you know, to put in my time, and it was kind of grim.

One Big Long Street

MINNIE IRVIN

on Courtship in Arrowhead

(RECORDED JUNE 2, 1964)

IN PRE-WAR British Columbia, many towns cropped up around natural resources such as mines, forests and fishing sites where canneries could be established. Men would flock to these centres in search of steady employment. In turn, women would follow. According to the 1911 census, males in British Columbia outnumbered females by two to one, but this number was drastically skewed in smaller industry-based locales.

Minnie Caldwell Irvin (née Smith, 1889–1968) describes her experience living in Arrowhead, a community located forty miles south of Revelstoke in the Kootenays. In 1895, the town was established as a steamboat port at the head of Upper Arrow Lake, one of two lakes situated between the Selkirk Mountains to the east and the Monashee Mountains to the west. The town served as the supply point for the lake and other sites nearby. Lumbering and mining were major industries in this part of the Kootenays, and with the CPR also passing through Arrowhead, the community thrived at the turn of the century. With industry petering out, Arrowhead was eventually abandoned in 1968 when the Hugh Keenleyside Dam became operational. As a consequence, the townsite is now mostly submerged beneath the lake.

Minnie describes meeting and marrying her husband Samuel Irvin. Their first child was born in Arrowhead, and then her husband took over the Coronation Hotel in Athalmer, where their twin girls were born. Two years later, in 1915, the family relocated to Rossland so her stepson could receive schooling. There, they purchased the Central Hotel and renamed it the Irvin Hotel, and the rest of their children were born in Rossland. At the time of this recording, Minnie was proud to proclaim that she made the right choice by marrying Samuel Irvin: "I have eight children, twenty-six grandchildren and thirteen great-grandchildren. And looking forward to a couple more." The Irvin Hotel was the only hotel in Rossland to survive the Great Depression. Minnie and Samuel Irvin operated that hotel until 1958, when they retired and moved to Chilliwack.

·   ·   ·

CD1, TRACK 5 MINNIE IRVIN: I was originally from Nova Scotia and came out to British Columbia in 1911. And my father and two brothers were here before me. And I visited a few days in Revelstoke and then went down to Arrowhead, where my brother and father were employed in the mill. Well, I left to come west. I was engaged to be married back there and thought it wise to do a little travelling first because I was afraid if I settled down I would be like a lot of the other Nova Scotian girls that I knew. I wouldn't get the chance to travel. So my brother sent me a good-sized cheque, and having my own little account, why, I made the trip quite nicely out here. My fiancé said to me when I was—it was a man whom I had never heard

The Irvin Hotel in Rossland, 1930s, which Minnie Irvin and her husband ran for over forty years. Photo: E-05329/Lythgoe

use a profane word of any kind—but he said, "Would you please tell me, what in hell made you make up your mind to go to British Columbia?" [laughs] And then I told him that I thought I'd better travel before getting married. [laughs]

When I arrived on the 10th day of February, the snow was terrific. We had snow in Nova Scotia but nothing to compare with the depth of snow in Revelstoke. And also in Arrowhead. Now my first impression, the first morning I got up and looked around was that I was so enclosed with mountains that I wondered how I would ever get out of them. There didn't look to be any way out, as there was no road except the railroad coming in to Arrowhead. But you soon overcome that, and I wouldn't change the mountains now for anything in the world.

I dearly loved Arrowhead. They were friendly people and there was one point that made it most interesting. I don't remember the exact number of male employees at the Lower Arrow Lakes Mill and the Big Ben Lumber Company across from the town. But my estimation would be that there were probably five or six hundred men working. And in all the town of Arrowhead, which was small, there were five unmarried girls. So a person had a choice of going where they liked and having what they liked, because you only had to mention that you liked a particular thing and you got entirely too much of it.

I had one little experience with burnt almond chocolate candies. I happened to mention to a bookkeeper from the mill that I was very fond of burnt almonds. His next trip to Revelstoke, he brought me a five-pound box of Mannings chocolates. A big red box with a red ribbon bow on it, and before that week was over I had five more boxes. And I don't ever want to see burnt almond chocolates again. Never did want to see them after that. [laughs] And they were the kindest class of people that anybody could meet. A wonderful class of people.

Now, experiences in that town were limited because you had just the railroad to walk up and down. You could take the boat, which there were many of them, for a very nominal sum, take a little trip down to Halcyon Hot Springs, which I think was a boat. Twenty miles from Arrowhead by boat, maybe more. And they had marvellous baths, marvellous attendants, and their dining room could not be excelled. Not even by the CPR.

Which was wonderful on the boats, too. And then for a day's outing you would go up to Revelstoke by train, twenty-eight miles, and you would do most of your shopping in Revelstoke, and there were good picture shows and that sort of thing in those days.

Arrowhead, as you came into it, had three lovely big hotels. The first one was the Union, run by Mr. and Mrs. Lakeburn. The next one was the City Hotel, and the Lakeview was owned and operated by my husband. A very lovely looking hotel with a lot of dormer windows at the top, and it was really a nice sight when you got off the boat coming up from that end of the town to see three such lovely hotels in such a small town. They were nicely run and as I said before, we didn't have the conveniences; we didn't have hot and cold water and that sort of thing. Lots of cold water, but not much hot. And we had a jewellery store and two clothing stores and there was a real good, as I remember it, a real good bakery and a real good butcher shop. But the town was just like one big long street. And when you got off that, it was just go straight up the hill or straight down. Because it was built right on the side of a mountain. Then the first year I was there, my husband asked me if I'd teach him to skate, which I did. In about three days, he was teaching me. [laughs] Although I'd always been a real good skater. And we skated one morning from—over the ice, on the lake—from Arrowhead into Comaplix, which was nine miles. We had our dinner at the Lardo Hotel in Comaplix and returned that afternoon, by ice, and that could— was quite a feat. [laughs] More tiring to me than it was to him. He had really mastered the art of skating in a very short time. I might say that I met him on Sunday at noon and was engaged to be married to him on Wednesday, and nineteen days later I married him. And made a very fine choice.

In Arrowhead, the main thing up there was the building of the railroad by Mackenzie, Mann and Company from Golden through to Cranbrook. And there was some

Halcyon Hot Springs, a favourite destination for the people of Arrowhead, 1920. Photo: E-09172

Skating in the Kootenays, ca. 1895. Minnie and Samuel Irvin's rapid courtship developed on the ice. Photo: A-02071

lumbering, some beautiful timber brought out of there, and the Paradise Mine was working. In my time, the railroads, of course, made it very, very busy because we were overtaxed to handle the work. In those days, they didn't have a great big bulldozer, that was all done with pick and shovel. And when you look back, it was quite a thing to compare that with what you see today. When you see one of these big shovels go in and take up the amount of earth and know what those men had to, and I was there at the laying of the ties and the rails. Every bit of it done by hand. A lot of it was Italian labour, but there was a lot of other labourers, too. Canadians.

After I came out, I didn't stay there very long. We only stayed two and a half years after I was married, but it wasn't too long after that that they had a disastrous fire at the mill, and that slowed the town down a lot. Then the Big Bend closed down across, and little by little, Arrowhead just gradually sort of faded. And today, I think there's only one, if there is one at all, there's only one hotel left. The other two burned down. And all the stores, there's just the one—there was one big store on the main street, there's just the odd building left. There are a few living there yet, and I suppose always will be.

(2)

When We Were Young

NEW TRANSPORTATION routes, such as the Canadian Pacific and Grand Trunk Pacific railways, made it easier to get the province's natural resources to market, and British Columbia's economy grew in the late 1800s and early 1900s. Newcomers increasingly had access to more locales, both remote outposts and an ever-increasing number of more established towns, and many of them started to build homes and settle permanently. The nomadic gold seekers moved on, and in their place came families with children.

Thousands of young children found themselves having to acclimatize to new and often unforgiving landscapes. For many, the ability to adapt meant the difference between a happy or difficult childhood. They were frequently given tremendous responsibilities and isolated from other kids. These three stories represent completely different experiences: Annie Levelton came into a thriving, tight-knit community; Pattie Haslam lived cut off from most people at a lighthouse; and Cecilia Bullen was born into one of British Columbia's most prominent early families. As each of them recalls her youth, she reconnects with and captures the innocence, spirit and wonder of her childhood.

FACING: *A Nuu-chah-nulth village scene, 1930.*
Photo: AA-00227/Doris Galligos

These Horses Came Towards Us

ANNIE LEVELTON

on Being Saved by Capoose

(RECORDED AUGUST 18, 1966)

SEVERAL FIRST Nations have inhabited the Bella Coola valley for 10,000 years, and traditionally the people who lived there were known by place names, such as Tallio. The first European contact in the area was on June 1, 1793, and the Hudson's Bay Company established its first trading post there in 1867, first on a boat and later on the south side of the river. Around this time, many First Nations in the valley began to congregate into large villages in an effort to combat the smallpox epidemic that was decimating the communities. By 1864, only a few hundred people were left.

Around this time, the people who lived at Bella Coola started to call themselves Nuxálk, which partially means "the place where fish were trapped." They adopted the name Bella Coola after the name of the river. Not only were the Nuxálk people trappers, they were intermediaries who controlled trade between the Interior and the coast. They carried furs up the river in canoes for trade with the Heiltsuk in Bella Bella.

The first influx of non-Native settlers occurred when the Nuxálk welcomed a group of Norwegians in 1893. Reverend Christian Saugstad, pastor of the Lutheran Free Church in Polk County, Minnesota, was the leader of the community. His parishioners did not feel at home on the prairies, and their wages were not enough to entice them to stay. Instead, they longed for a place that would remind them of Norway. The long fjord and steep mountains around Bella Coola felt right, and so they built their community there and called it Hagensborg.

FACING: *Reverend Christian Saugstad led his parishioners*
from Minnesota to Bella Coola, which reminded them of their
native Norway. Photo: B-00597

Rasmus Levelton (1855–1944) was from Embardo, Norway, and had barely settled in Minnesota when he made the trip to the Bella Coola Valley to set up a cabin, a year before his family moved. His daughter Annie Helene Levelton (1891–1971) was only 4 years old when she arrived on May 6, 1895. This interview gives us a very interesting window into what it would have been like to be a young girl arriving on the west coast of Canada in the late 1890s.

·　　·　　·

CD1, TRACK 6 ANNIE LEVELTON: I can just remember the sensation I had when they— when some officer or my father—I'm not sure who it was that picked me up and put me over the rail of the ship as we arrived— You know, I mean to say there wasn't any wharf to come to, you know? And, we were— it was in a dugout canoe—well, I had never seen an Indian or a canoe in my life, you know, I was only 4. Well, you might know what the— I don't think I yelled even. I was too scared to even yell. But I can just remember coming up by canoe again from Claytons. Claytons, that was Hudson Bay, and up as far as, oh, about two miles down here. And I can remember walking from that canoe and up here, that is as much as I can remember of that day. But father had a cabin, luckily. He was the only one that really had a good cabin and, and so we had a home to go to, but it was alarming after being on the prairie to see all those huge trees, you know?

Father left Minnesota in the fall and got here on the 30th of October. Whereas we didn't arrive till the next year in May; on May the 6th we arrived in Bella Coola. Father came in '94. He went ahead to build a cabin and have everything ready till we arrived, you see. He travelled with Mr. Saugstad, Reverend Saugstad, who was the leader of the band that came out here, and that is how we were a year late. Well, I don't remember the dimensions of the cabin, but it was one of the biggest cabins in the valley at that time. And how Father ever built that cabin, I will never know. They didn't have all the facilities for all these things as yet, but he was a marvellous broad axe man. And there wasn't many other good broad axe men in the valley, and three of them, you see, that when they came in here, they took the— the three men went together. And they

The Bella Coola Valley. Photo: E-01939

built cabins as they went along, you know. Because they couldn't do it by themselves.

You know, some of those people over there, well, they weren't too badly off because they sold farms and made about $5,000 or $6,000 at least for the farm, and we didn't have that. We just didn't. Well, there weren't too many people moving in, you see. The lot that started from Minnesota, that eighty that started out, forty went back of that lot. They didn't stay at all. They decided that it was too rugged for them so they just took off and waited for six weeks or whatever it was for the next boat to come. But I can remember as a little girl, that Mr. Clayton used to have my father down there to do his carpentry work a lot. And so, that paid off a lot of our bills and we used to get our clothing from Mrs. Clayton.

Well, the Indians were surprisingly very good to us. They could have resented us pretty badly, but they were awfully good to us. And we were

Members of the Nuxálk First Nation, 1885. Photo: B-03826/Carl Gunther

good to them. The settlers, I will say this, I'll pay a tribute to the settlers and say that they were fine men. Some of them would talk Norski, and the Indians would talk Indian language and seem to understand each other very well. I never did know how they did it, but, anyway, that's the way of life, you know?

My life was saved by one of them, and I just loved him till the day of his death. He was the, one of the chiefs of the, or second in command, I believe, at Anahim Lake. His name was Capoose, and Capoose was quite a famous man. He would, he would never dress as an Indian, you know. He copied one of our Englishmen who arrived from the Boer War, you know. After the Boer War he came out here and he wore all the whole regalia of the riding pants and the white shirt and the Stetson hats, and oh, he was the most immaculate-looking creature you ever saw. Mustache and all. And Capoose imitated that dress and I don't think he wore anything else. Never down here, at least, he didn't. He'd always say, "Me all the same white man now." That was it.

But the first time, my introduction to Capoose, I must tell you about was rather a— could have been a— rather a tragic one for me. Oh, I suppose I was about 5 at the time and my brother and I, we heard this tinking of bells. Well, anything on the road in those days was news to us. We had to see what it was, naturally. And we stood out by the road and this—it was about, oh, just a little ways down here, the trail went in, and these horses came towards us, and when the horses saw us, I— and we kind of backed off the road then, and we started to run up towards our cabin. And the horses followed us. And they were running so fast and

The infamous Capoose (far left), 1928, was a Nuxálk chief who saved 5-year-old Annie Levelton from being trampled by horses. Photo: H-06526/Frank Cyril Swannell

me— I stumbled and fell right in front of them. And this fellow, this same Capoose, spurred his horse on and he just bent down and he grabbed me by whatever clothing he could find and hauled me up onto the pommel of the saddle and took me to my mother. Well, he saved my life. Those horses would have stepped on me, no doubt about it, because they'd be crowded in on that path, you know. They wouldn't have wanted to do it, but the horse will if he can't find anywheres else to stand, he's got to stand on something. So, anyway, I thought Capoose was a pretty nice fellow after that. I just thought he was just wonderful. So we'd watch for Capoose, we'd watch for his pack train and every year just as regular as clockwork, we'd be out there to see old Capoose come down.

Waiting to Hear the Tom-Toms

PATTIE HASLAM

on Living at Cape Beale Lighthouse

RECORDED MARCH 26, 1962

PATTIE ALEXANDER Haslam (née Cox, 1875–1974) was the daughter of Emmanuel and Frances Cox. Emmanuel Cox was overseer of Lord Hamilton's estate in County Cork, Ireland. Wishing to escape class distinctions, he and his wife immigrated to California. Upon hearing word that Vancouver Island had a landscape and climate similar to Ireland's, the Coxes moved north in the early 1870s and Emmanuel found work as an agricultural labourer. When Lord Hamilton, along with Lord and Lady Dufferin, visited Vancouver Island in 1874, they sought out Emmanuel and were appalled to see him living life as a labourer. Lady Dufferin used her political influence to secure a job for him as a lighthouse keeper on Berens Island in Victoria Harbour. Pattie was born there.

Three years later, in 1878, the family—which now included five children (Pattie, Frances, Annie, Gus and Ernest)—moved to the Cape Beale lighthouse on the west coast of Vancouver Island. That lighthouse is best known for its proximity to the West Coast Trail, a trail forged by survivors of the many shipwrecks along this rocky coast to get to the nearby community of Bamfield. In Patttie's day, the lighthouse consisted of a keeper's house and a thirty-one-foot tapered tower, which was painted white and topped by a black lantern room. The family lived in total isolation from other settlers, receiving supplies via a government boat that visited twice a year. Pattie, therefore, had a very "quiet" childhood except for the three years she spent at school in Victoria.

Over the course of this interview, Pattie often refers to the "Indians." These are various members of the Nuu-chah-nulth First Nations who have inhabited the area around Cape Beale for more than 4,000 years. She also refers to a potlatch ceremony, the gift-giving feast practised by many First Nations of the Northwest Coast to celebrate births, deaths, adoptions, weddings and other major events. The word comes from the Chinook jargon meaning "to give away" or "a gift," and it is a custom at potlatches to give many ceremonial gifts. The ritual is a vital part of the traditional economic system. Many potlatches took years to prepare, even though the actual event would only last four or five days. In 1884, both the Canadian and US governments banned potlatches believing that the act of giving away one's hard-earned possessions was in opposition to capitalist values; however, many continued in secret. The ban was repealed in 1951.

.   .   .

CD1, TRACK 7 PATTIE HASLAM: The only part of going to Cape Beale that I remember—of course I was only 3 years old—we had to go up a trail to the lighthouse that was quite steep. I wasn't able to walk, it was very rough, and there was an Indian with us, that brought us there, I presume. And his name was Whiskey Charlie. A very handsome Indian. And he kept saying to me, "Put your arms around my neck." He had me on his back, you know, carrying me up this steep trail. It was the mainland when the tide was out, but when the tide came in it was an island. But, of course, when the tide was out there was lots of pools there with salt water, an excellent place for bathing. Sandy beaches, you know, and we could play about there. It was an ideal life, really. No chance of getting into any mischief or trouble, just lived our life apart from everybody.

Of course, we had a herd of goats there, which provided milk and fresh meat. It was impossible to get along on bacon and salt meat all the time, which they had to order about six months ahead of time. And not only the supply for ourselves, but in case of the shipwrecked men and all that sort of thing.

We stayed at Cape Beale, Mother taught us— and my sister and I, my sister Annie and I, until we were about 10 years old. And then we were

Pattie Haslam spent a quiet childhood in the Cape Beale lighthouse on the west coast of Vancouver Island.
Photo: B-06175

sent to Victoria and we went to the Cridge's private school. Our life in Victoria, of course, was all study until we, I think we were here about two or three years, then went back to the lighthouse, Cape Beale. And Mother continued our studies. Not only in teaching, deportment, lessons of one thing or another. And also our life. She never failed on that. With the happy result that we can go anywhere now, meet anywhere—always have been able to do it—and know how to behave.

She had a garden, she worked hard in it, my father dug it for her, she did the planting. And she spent a good deal of time with it. She did wonderful needlework, all that sort of thing. But she never once, that I ever heard, complained of the lonely life. In fact, she liked it. If we complained, she'd say very quietly, "Oh dear, do be quiet. Everything's all right."

There were lots of the Indians about there. They were the Huu-ay-aht tribe, and the men—that's the elderly men—all wore their hair long, and bound round tight in a bun, with cedar bark at the back of their head. The young men usually wore a, oh, I suppose you'd call it a bandeau around their head, a handkerchief folded, one of the large red type. The women, they had beautiful long black hair, and in those days, they used to decorate their hair with thimbles, made like bells. Oh, there must have

Members of the Nuu-chah-nulth First Nation flensing a whale on the beach, 1907.
Photo: AA-00038/Moser

been about a dozen on the end of each braid. And every time they moved their head, these thimbles would tinkle like bells. But they were always very modest, carefully dressed, and very shy as a rule.

Yes, we saw them whaling—but they had great large war canoes, beautiful things. It would hold about six men, there'd be three seats, and two men on each seat. And then the man in the stern steering, and one in the bow. And they always kept perfect rhythm. All the spears had great large floats, bladders on the end, and these spears would go right into them, you see, and the blubber bladders would keep the whale afloat.

Then they would fasten a rope to the whale, and they brought it in between these war canoes. Sometimes there was two, and sometimes four. It was quite a sight. And the war canoe leading had the drum. And they beat the drum and chanted over the bay, oh, well, whenever they came within distance of the lighthouse. And they'd all go away down Barkley Sound to their village.

But on one occasion, a storm came up, and they brought the wretched thing into the entrance at Cape Beale lighthouse. There was a gap, you know, where a rowboat could come in to land our supplies at the lighthouse. And they brought this whale in, and got it up on the beach. And then, after they had brought it in, they went up to ask my father if he objected to them bringing it in there. Well, he ordered them to take it out. Take it away. And oh, they were going to cut it up, and they take it home in pieces, and you know, the thing was there for weeks. There was an awful fuss about it, because it smelt so badly. You know, they got an awful odour. Anyway, they cut it up. What we did, us children went down to see this whale after they brought it in. And then when they got this poor creature home, they'd have another celebration. A sort of a feast. It wasn't a potlatch.

But these Nitinat Indians, one time, there was some of them passing through to what they called a potlatch, that was given by other Indians at Dodger's Cove. That was where the schooners used to anchor when they were not sealing. It's about three miles from Cape Beale. When they gave these potlatches, well, that was about the only thing we ever went to. We used to go to watch them dance. You know, they dance very nicely, though in the Indian fashion, of course.

Gift-giving at potlatch ceremonies formed a vital part of the traditional cultural and economic systems of many First Nations of the Northwest Coast, 1866–70. Photo: C-09283/Frederick Dally

Well, the potlatch, as far as the Indians were concerned, was a very joyous affair. One Indian and his klootchman would give the potlatch, which meant that the whole entertainment was provided by them alone. And they had saved up for six months, or maybe longer, shawls and food and baskets, and all sorts of things. And then three Indians would beat the tom-tom. That's their drum, which is deerskin, but drawn tightly over hoops and laced at the back with strings. It makes a very good drum-like sound. They would play, and these Indians would have a great large fire in the centre of the Indian house, which was the largest that could be found, and they danced all around this, chanting as they danced. But they always keep perfect time, and sing very nicely. Nearly all the Indians have very good singing voices. Melodious, you know. And they'd chant away, and when all these goods that had been provided, sometimes a box of pilot bread, all sorts— Pounds of tea, anything that they could get that would please these friends that they had invited, they would give away at this dance. But they never give anything to people that were visiting, like my sister Annie and I. And then, to prevent the house filling with smoke from this open fire they'd have in the centre of the room, they'd have a hole cut in the roof, so the smoke can go out. And then all around the building, there was the flat platform, like, where they sleep at night. They never have any bedding, you know, really. They just sleep on the— oh, take a blanket and roll up in it, maybe a cedar mat on the, over the bare boards, but they never have any mattress or anything like that. Oh, it was quite interesting to see their way of life; it's so entirely different from anything of our own.

But my sister and I did have a very pleasant trip to Victoria when Captain Jacobson and his wife came down the west coast on a sealing trip. Well, when the captain got his catch, he used to return with them to Dodger's Cove, where his wife had a house. And he'd store the catch there—which she looked after, for fear of theft or anything of that sort. And when she got the opportunity, she came over to see Mother. And got very well acquainted with her, very nice person. She was a Miss McLean of Victoria. And, well, after she had been at the lighthouse to see Mother, she invited my sister Annie and I to come back with her on the sealing schooner when they were returning to Victoria. Which we did. And it was a great pleasure indeed watching all these sailing schooners going along Barkley Sound out to sea with their Indian hunters going catching seals. Oh my, must be, it was a good deal over seventy years ago. We had a very jolly time onboard. My sister played the accordion, went dancing nearly every evening, and we got to Victoria. We were to stay about a week. Well, the return trip I never heard anything about. I don't know how we were supposed to get back because the government boat with supplies only went every six months.

However, we were in town one day and going around shopping and looking at the shops, one thing and another, and we met an Indian and his wife. His name was Dick Clamhouse, and we asked him when he was returning and he said, oh, he'd come over to Captain Jacobson's schooner and tell us when he was going. Which he did, and he was returning by canoe. Captain Jacobson asked him if he could take us back home and he said, "Yes." Now he was the mail carrier from Cape Beale to Alberni. He was to take the mail once a month and that was, from Cape Beale to Alberni is thirty-nine miles. And he used to be paid $5 a month by the government to do this. Well, to get back to the trip, he said he'd be leaving Captain Jacobson's schooner about nine in the morning and we were to be there to meet him, but we had to work our way for the trip back home to Cape Beale. So we said all right.

Mrs. Jacobson gave us each a blanket and a supply of food that would last about three days, and the canoe was about twenty-five feet long. And you know they're very narrow, there's just only a width in the bottom of the canoe for my sister and I to sit together. And with the food and their baggage and supplies that they had been buying, you couldn't sit anyway but tail wise, you know? With [laughs] the result quite often when we did stand up to get out of the canoe, we couldn't walk. But, however, we left Victoria that morning about nine o'clock or shortly after, and it took us four days and three nights to get from Victoria to Cape Beale. With just my sister and I and the Indian and his wife. We went ashore occasionally at different beaches all the ways to exercise and get fresh water, which he brought in a sort of a large jar I suppose you'd call it.

Everything was all right until we got to Nitinat, which I think is about halfway between Victoria and Cape Beale. And we were going in there at night—it was dark—and my sister and I were talking and laughing about different things. And he said, *"Tlush vash mika halo wawa. Nika delate kwass."* That was "Please don't talk, I'm very much afraid." Well of course, that startled my sister and I. So when we got in— it's gently, he wouldn't let us paddle even. The canoe touched the beach, he told us to get out quietly. We went back to the canoe, my sister did, and asked him what was the matter. She wanted to know. And he said he wanted to keep as far away from the village as he possibly could because he had fallen in love with the chief's daughter who wouldn't allow him to marry her because she was much superior being the chief's daughter, and he'd just simply sneaked around at night, captured her and took her off. And he was afraid if the chief caught him there that night that he would murder the whole lot of us. Well, you can imagine what a quiet, nice night we had. [laughs] With the anticipation of being murdered. However, he said that we were to take the cedar mat; we were not to go far from the canoe. We used to go up a piece to get away from the damn sand. We were to stay close to the canoe, and if we heard the Indian tom-toms beating, we were to come and wake him and his wife, he'll push off the canoe and leave at once. But for us to take the cedar mat with us. [laughs] Well, we didn't sleep that night. We were waiting to hear the tom-toms, but they didn't come. No, I don't think the Indians knew that we were there.

So we continued on our tiresome journey until we got to Cape Beale, landing at many different points, you know. There was no— of course if the wind or the weather had any appearance of becoming rough, we would go in and stay in till it got calmer, then start off again. Quite often we sailed and then had a rest from the continuing paddling. And apart from that, I think, the trip was quite uneventful.

A House Full of People

on Saturday Nights at Helmcken House

(RECORDED IN MARCH 1962)

CECILIA MARY Bullen (b. 1889) was born in Victoria to James Douglas Helmcken and Ethyl Margaret Mouat. She is the granddaughter of two of British Columbia's first non-Native settlers. Her maternal grandfather was Captain William Alexander Mouat, who was born in 1821 in London, England. In 1844, Mouat served as the second mate on the Hudson's Bay Company's steamship *Vancouver*, before being sent to New Caledonia (the region that would later be known as British Columbia) in 1849. In fact, he was charged with establishing Fort Rupert, which is now known as Port Hardy, on the northern tip of Vancouver Island. He married Maryann Ainsley in 1854, and the couple, along with their seven children, were posted back to Fort Rupert in 1866. The only other non-Native person there was the Roman Catholic priest. Without a doctor nearby, they lost one daughter before Captain Mouat died of a heart attack while out in a canoe in 1871. His widow, Maryann, had to wait until a ship came up and took word back to Victoria that her husband had died. Then the ship had to return and take her children and all of their belongings back to Victoria, which is where she eventually died.

Cecilia Bullen's paternal grandfather, John Sebastian Helmcken, was the first physician posted to Vancouver Island. Born in 1824, Helmcken was of German descent, but born in England. Among other exploits, he travelled to India as a medical officer. He first arrived on Vancouver Island in 1850, eight years before the first gold rush brought the first

57

Dr. John Sebastian Helmcken, Vancouver Island's first physician, ca. 1895.
Photo: A-01349/John Savannah

huge wave of immigrants, and a couple hundred non-Native people were living on the island at that time. Besides being a surgeon, Dr. Helmcken was one of three negotiators who brought British Columbia into Confederation.

In this anecdote, Cecilia mentions that her grandfather married one of the Douglases. James Douglas was the chief factor of the Hudson's Bay Company and second governor of the Crown Colony of Vancouver Island. After Douglas appointed Helmcken as the surgeon to the jail in the Fort Victoria Bastions in 1850, he asked Helmcken to marry his eldest daughter, Cecilia, which solidified the bonds between these two families and ensured that Helmcken settled in Victoria, where he remained until his death in September 1920.

The Helmckens' family life centred around the home that Dr. Helmcken had built in 1852. To this day, Helmcken House is located on the grounds of the Royal British Columbia Museum in Victoria and it is still a major tourist attraction. Cecilia Bullen would have spent a lot of time in that house as a little girl and offers details about her grandfather and life in this famous home.

·   ·   ·

CD1, TRACK 8 CECILIA BULLEN: My name was Helmcken, and my grandfather was the first doctor here, you see. But still, our people really played a great part in the beginning of Victoria, naturally. Grandfather Helmcken, you see Grandfather died only in 1919, I think it was. And he really had a very colourful life. He was really quite a character, he had a great sense of humour, was a frightfully hospitable man, imaginable. Very casual with his bills and that sort of thing. With people my father was the same, he was a doctor too. [laughs] If people didn't pay their bills, "Oh well, poor things, they can't help it!" you know, that sort of way. So neither of them were ever rich from their profession. [laughs]

But Grandfather, really, was quite a character. He was, for years, doctor to the jail in Victoria, and he had great affection for some of the old jailbirds. He was just awfully good to them. In fact, he was too good to them. And there were two old characters who used to come. They'd be taken in in the winter, you see, to give them a home, and they had to do certain jobs around the place. Then, in the summer, they were turned loose again, you see? And then, every day, they would come to Grandfather, and Grandfather had an old Chinese cook—been with him for years—and he would come in and say, "Skat!" which meant Scott, who was one of the men, and the other was Grayson. And my aunt, who was a widow and lived with him, would be so angry with him, because he always kept rolls and rolls of 25¢ pieces in a desk and he'd say, "Doll, give Scott a quarter." "Father, you gave him a quarter yesterday; he doesn't need it today." "Give Scott a quarter." So, then, Scott would get his quarter. The next day it would be Grayson, you see. This went on year after year for ages in the summer, of course. But I think he really got quite, had quite an affection for them. He used to say, "Oh, Scott's not a bad chap. He doesn't steal, he only gets tight." [laughs] Very tolerant.

Grandfather came in 1850. I often wonder how they got horses and buggies here, because grandfather had a tremendously high old buggy and a horse named Bob. And then he had to ride too, because there were not very many streets in which they could take a horse and trap of any sort. But he had to ride, and, of course, it was all forest all about there. But you know Helmcken House, don't you? And that, of course, the original bit of it, was built for him and for his bride, who was one of the Douglases. She was Cecilia Douglas. And that is their mansion they lived in. And then as the family grew, they had to add a bit, you see, and then they had to add another bit. [laughs] Consequently it's a very odd-looking place now, but the original part is quite of interest.

It was always full of people. My aunt was as hospitable, if not more so, than Grandfather. And she always had a tremendous number of visitors. And Grandfather liked to entertain: he wasn't so keen on having just one or two people, but he liked to have a house full of people always. And one funny characteristic he had: Saturday night. He expected all his

Mrs. Cecilia Helmcken, née Douglas, before 1865. Photo: A-01682

relations, his family, to gather round him on Saturday night. As we'd grow old it got to be a little bit of a bore, I don't mind telling you, but Saturday night had to be kept for Grandfather. And we had music, we sat around the piano. And he always had whist, certain old cronies who came to play, to play whist with him always. And we used to be very much amused as he got older and older, and the grandsons got a bit bored with it every Saturday night, you see, and they used to try to hurry the game through. And Grandfather would say, "Damn it all, don't you know I can see through you?" [laughs] "You needn't think that I can't play this game!" [laughs] And we can hear this all over the house; it was frightfully funny.

IMBERT ORCHARD: Were you in another room?

BULLEN: Yes, generally. Oh yes, yes, we...

ORCHARD: The music went on in another room.

BULLEN: Oh yes, the music went on in another room. Oh well, as time went on, of course, it developed into a more modern type, but we used to sing things like, oh, "Swanee River" and "Old Uncle Ned" and "Annie Laurie," and you know, that type of music. And if anybody came along who was musical and wanted to sing, well, they sat down and they had a turn at it too.

Well, are you interested in hearing about his Christmas dinner? Because that really was something. It was a family dinner always, you see, and always twenty or more sat down to this enormous great table. Each family—you see, in those days we all had Chinese cooks—so each family sent the cook ahead to help get the dinner, you see. And Grandfather, of course, had a Chinese cook. And then they all waited at the table afterwards. And the dinner was simply, I don't know, I think you'd call it prodigious. How we ever got through it, I don't know. [laughs] But we always started off with oyster patties. Now, nowadays, when you get an oyster patty, it's a little thing like that. But it used to be a thing about like that, colossal. And then we had soup, and then we had— on came an enormous roast turkey and a goose—and, I think, and one of the relations the other day said, "Weren't there two turkeys?" and I think there were—and then there was chicken and, of course, ham and tongue and various things to go with it. Mountains of vegetables came round. And then we had plum pudding and great big mince tarts—enormous, big things. And fruit of all sorts. Dried fruits, namely.

And then came the toasts. And Grandfather, first of all, would

The dining room in Helmcken House. Photo: C-08300

Left to right: Dr. Jim Helmcken with baby Edith Helmcken; Mrs. Edward Gordon; Edward Gordon holding Eric; Cecilia, seated on a stool; and Mrs. Jim Helmcken, 1895. Photo: B-03634

propose the toast to the Queen. And then we all had to stand for the Queen. And then somebody would propose Grandfather's health, a host. And then Grandfather would reply. And then somebody would propose the toast to my aunt, who had all of the arranging to do, you see. And then she would always just bow, but she never made any talk. And then it went round the table, toasts to everybody. [laughs] It really was very funny, quite amusing. But we turned and got awfully bored with it, you see, when we were very young, so half the time we were always sent away from the table and allowed to race up and down the hall. [laughs] Work off our sort of irritation at having to sit for so long. Then, of course, we had bonbons, crackers, you know, and candies and things. Then we all adjourned to the drawing room, where we had music. And then we had a Christmas tree. We were called back after the table was cleared—we were called back to the dining room—and there was a colossal Christmas tree for us. And then the Christmas tree was pushed into another room, and then we had to dance. I'll tell you, it was quite a night. How the mothers survived, I don't know. [laughs]

But my last, my last Christmas there was Christmas of 1918, at the end of the war. I got back from England, I had been in England; my husband was over there. And I came back from England, and I had my small boy who was then 11 months old. And that was the last Christmas dinner that Grandfather could have. After that, well, he was too old and he died at the age— He was in his ninety-seventh year when he died, you see. But I was always glad to be able to tell my son that he was at a Christmas dinner, not that he knew anything about it because he slept all the time. [laughs] But it was interesting to know that he was there. But really, the days were lovely, I think, in those days, much more natural, somehow or other. We didn't make the fuss over things that we do nowadays, you know, entertaining and that sort of thing. People came, and you were so glad to see them, and you gave them just what was there, and they were happy about it. But nowadays, if you know somebody's coming, what a fuss we make about it, cutting sandwiches and doing all sorts of silly things. I do it all the time, I know. [laughs]

Mischief and Mayhem

B RITISH COLUMBIA is four times the size of Great Britain, but in 1900 the total population of the province was just 170,000 people, or about three of every hundred people living in Canada. All that open space with so few people living on it meant there was lots of mischief to be had.

To be sure, even for those who did not seek it out, everyday life seemed to involve its good share of mayhem, especially for those outside of the few cities. Many immigrants were inexperienced living in extreme wilderness, and there were few systems in place to help people adapt to ever-changing conditions. It is also true that unpredictability bred resourcefulness and a dependence on others. In these environments, playful mischief could take the edge off difficult times and could also help build friendships.

FACING: *The infamous Simon Gunanoot (left) at the Hazelton cemetery, 1920. Photo: A-07788*

As these stories show, the mayhem ranged from playful pranks to murder. The latter was infrequent in British Columbia's early days, as Sir Matthew Baillie Begbie (1819–1894), the province's first official judge appointed in 1858, decreed that the death penalty be mandatory in murder cases. This precedent, and the fact that he ordered fifty-two hangings during his tenure—thereby giving him the nickname of The Hanging Judge—ensured that by the turn of the century, British Columbia was perceived as a safe place to settle. Be that as it may, when murder did occur, it could divide a community or sometimes, surprisingly, bring it together.

You Mutton-Headed Chumps

FLORENCE TRUDEAU

on Racing Horses While Standing Up

(RECORDED JULY 20, 1968)

———

KNOWN AS "Bunch" to her friends and family, Florence Lytle Trudeau (1918–2006) was born in Montana and moved to Canada with her family when she was 9 months old. She was the youngest of four children; her siblings were Jane, Caroline and Alfred. Her parents Cyrus and Phyllis Bryant settled at Tatla Lake, 220 kilometres west of Williams Lake on the western edge of the Chilcotin Plateau. In fact, some of the largest mountains in British Columbia are found there, including Mount Waddington, which is the tallest mountain entirely within the province's borders.

Growing up in such isolation, Bunch's only playmates were her animals and siblings. Since there was so much to do to maintain the property and keep the family fed, the children were entrusted with chores from the time they could walk, including filling coal-oil lamps, gardening and helping with the canning for winter. Their parents also supplied them with lots of books. The kids would pretend to be knights and play intricate games based on these stories. In fact, the kids would fashion shields and armour from the bark of nearby poplar trees. The family also kept a 200-pound moose calf as a pet.

The following story highlights the tight bond Bunch shared with her brother, Alfred, and with her parents. It was her father who taught her how to swing an axe and how to cook. These kids used their animals as sources of mischief, but their parents' supportive and watchful eyes were never far behind.

· · ·

CD2, TRACK 1 FLORENCE TRUDEAU: Why, yes, I was only 9 months old as far as Mother's— so Mother told me. What she's told about, she used to have to take my bottle up to the— she'd give it to the conductor and he'd take it up to the engine and warm it for me. [laughs]

I remember playing with rocks. And we find out now that we were playing with a gold nugget and didn't know it. The kids saw one later on, Alfred and Jane. But we were just playing. You know, it was— we were ranching— and rocks were our stock. But then I don't remember anything then until we started on the trip up to Tatla Lake. It seems to me now that we must have been living there so that Dad could go out and scout around and find a pre-emption. He wanted to pre-empt a place in BC. And he had to make a trip and find out where he wanted to locate. That's as near as I can gather now. But I know he went up beforehand, before we moved into the Tatla Lake country. He went up and he built a cabin. I believe I was 5.

Then he taught me, Daddy taught me how to use an axe. Oh. Then he brought me home a puppy when I was there that winter. That was Gus, half Doberman pinscher and half German shepherd, the most intelligent

A ranch on the Cariboo Wagon Road. Photo: D-03962

dog. I think it was one of the most intelligent dogs that was ever born. So he was my playmate. I taught him everything I could think of, and he sure—he learned—what I didn't teach him he picked up.

And then Alfred came back, and I was still going to school. I was riding two miles down to Tatla Lake to go to school. And I'd take my lunch and some hay behind my saddle and ride down there. But Dad wasn't home. He'd gone somewhere, and just my granddad. But Alfred and I wanted to go chase some wild horses. So I'd pretend to get ready to go to school, you see. And he'd start off quite early to go out chasing wild horses, you see, or out someplace that we told Grandpa. Then I'd start off for school and I'd pack a little extra lunch, you know. And then I'd meet Alfred— then we'd go out chasing wild horses.

Well, we got in one bunch and we saved two of them out and turned the rest out. And then our neighbours came up. And they heard we got these horses. Our neighbours came up and tried to claim them. So Grandpa wouldn't— Daddy was gone and Grandpa wouldn't let us keep them because it might cause trouble, so we turned them out. I'm mad we turned them out. We never got any wild horses out of that bunch. But Alfred and I kicked around an awful lot together. And then we decided we were going to learn to stand up and ride our horses, Alfred and I. I've seen him fall off eighteen times in about 200 yards. But we both learned to do it.

IMBERT ORCHARD: You mean stand on top of the horse?

TRUDEAU: Stand up on the horse, bareback, no saddle on, you know, and race them. Well, we got reasonably good at it, you know. And one time we were up at the— haying at the— oh, it was Jack's place, I guess it was, Alfred and I and Daddy. Daddy's riding the team behind. Of course, Alfred and I had our saddle horses. We had to have some class, you know, but bareback, of course. So we're coming down this meadow towards home that night and Alfred says, "See that white rock down there, Bunch?" And I said, "Yeah." He says, "I'll race you to it standing up." "Okay." And I turned to Daddy, I said, "You say go." He said, "You mutton-headed chumps. You're going to get killed one of these days. All right, go." And away we went.

Growing up on an isolated ranch, Bunch Trudeau spent most of her time with her siblings and animals, sometimes chasing wild horses with her brother when she was meant to be in school. Photo: B-03881

Well, Alfred's horse, he was a miserable little cuss. And he had a grand habit of when he started to run, just run a little ways and then suddenly he'd stop and he'd turn at right angles. Well, that doesn't go very good for standing up. And this is what he did. And Alfred, instead of falling flat, he landed running. And I was ahead. My horse was faster anyway. And I was ahead of him. And I was looking back and laughing at him, and suddenly my horse shied at the white rock. I had reached it and I didn't— I had forgot. And I landed flat on my stomach and just skidded like a skidder—a sled runner, you know. All the wind knocked out of me, and I can still see Daddy coming down the meadow as fast as he could make the old horses trot, you know, and jumping off and picking me up and saying, "You mutton-headed chump, how many times you going to scare your old pa to death?" Oh, gee.

Dead Men Tell No Tales

BERT GLASSEY

on the Real Story of Simon Gunanoot
and the Murder of Max Leclair

(RECORDED JUNE 28, 1961)

JOSEPH HERBERT Francis Glassey (1882–1962), or Bert as his friends called him, was born in St. Joseph's Hospital in Victoria, the first child born at the new facility. He moved to San Diego after finishing college in Victoria, then eventually moved to 150 Mile House in 1903. When rumours began of the "all red route" (the beginning of the building of the Grand Trunk Pacific Railway) going from east to west, Glassey decided to go and be a part of the action. With no roads going into the north, he arrived in Hazelton via the Telegraph Trail in 1904. He was working as a blacksmith in June 1906, the night Max Leclair was killed by Simon Gunanoot.

Simon Gunanoot was a prosperous Gitxsan merchant in the Kispiox Valley who lived with his wife and children on a large ranch. According to the proper historical record, on that June night, he and his brother-in-law Peter Himadam stopped at a roadhouse at Two Mile, near Hazelton. Gunanoot and Himadam got into an argument and eventually a fight with a dockworker named Alex McIntosh and a hunting guide named Max Leclair. Upon leaving the roadhouse, Gunanoot declared that he was "going to get a gun and fix him [Leclair]." The shot-up bodies of McIntosh and Leclair were found on the trail a few hours later.

Shortly thereafter a search party was assembled, and a reward of $1,000 was offered for the capture of Gunanoot and Himadam.

The search lasted thirteen years and cost the government more than $100,000. Even the Pinkerton Agency, the people who caught Jesse James, could not find Gunanoot.

In this interview, Bert Glassey refutes the historical record that Max Leclair was killed because he had crossed Simon Gunanoot. He argues that Max Leclair was simply in the wrong place at the wrong time.

. . .

CD2, TRACK 2

BERT GLASSEY: I was in Hazelton at the time, and there's been a great many stories about Simon Gunanoot, and Max Leclair is one of the troubles of Simon Gunanoot, which was absolutely in error. Leclair had come up there with some horses from the Cariboo, and he was to take a man by the name of R.J. Cowan out for big-game hunting, along with his party. And Max Leclair had come into Hazelton the day before, and had gone up to Glen Vowell. That was right near where Simon Gunanoot's family was living and himself. I agreed to shoe three of his horses, and he brought two of them in that morning, and I've always had the opinion, I'm always of that opinion. Max was coming—Max Leclair was coming into Hazelton for me to shoe these horses. In the meantime, Simon Gunanoot had had this trouble at Two Mile Creek with Angus McIntosh, and he came home and got his gun, went back and just as he came out onto the road from a trail onto the road going to the hospital, he met McIntosh, and turned around and shot him. Max Leclair was coming into Hazelton with the horses for me to shoe, and there was a hill, quite a little pitch on a steep grade. Well, he was coming up the hill, leading these horses, and riding one, and Simon Gunanoot had come over the top of the hill, was coming down. As he came down the

Simon Gunanoot, a merchant-turned-murderer who spent thirteen years in hiding, ca. 1930. Photo: A-04796

hill, this steep grade, he ran into Leclair. Well, Leclair saw him, and Gunanoot, after he passed him, thought, "Well, here they'll find McIntosh's body. Leclair will tell them in town that he saw me, and I'll just turn around and kill him." He turned around and shot him right in the cantle of the saddle, and Leclair dropped dead right there. And he went on. Well, there was a case of dead man tell no tales. Now, Leclair was innocent as far as Gunanoot's family was concerned. But, the history went on to repeat Leclair was in this mix-up. He was not.

Well, then, Alec Horner was on his way in from Kispiox, and he'd come in and forded the river, and was walking into town when he ran across Leclair's body, and just about two miles from Hazelton then. So he came in to Hazelton to report it, that he'd found Leclair's body out there. And he'd been shot—the word came in then that McIntosh had been shot. So Kirby, who was the constable at that time, Kirby took charge. We then decided that there was Peter Himadam, who was a brother-in-law of Simon Gunanoot's. Peter

Max Leclair was shot down by Simon Gunanoot in 1906. Bert Glassey maintains that Leclair was merely at the wrong place at the wrong time. Photo: D-00282

Himadam was along with him, but he wasn't mixed up in the fight at Two Mile Creek at all. But he got frightened, and he went off with Simon Gunanoot. But he was innocent of anything. But he was with Simon, and stayed with Simon for years. So when we got around with Constable Kirby, we formed a delegation to go up to bring Gunanoot in, and they swore in a number of us. They went up to get Gunanoot but they couldn't get him.

But they took his father. They brought his father in as hostage. Brought him in, and put him in the jail. Kept him in there, thinking that Simon would come in and give himself up, and they'd let the old man loose. Well, they put him in the jail, and Jay Bashman was sworn in, he was an old-timer around there. Jay was sworn in as a special constable to look after him. In those days, facilties weren't the best, especially out-door. The Native had to go to the toilet, so Jay took him down the street to where the Hazelton Hotel was. And in the back of the hotel was the privy. So Jay sent Simon Gunanoot's father in there to the toilet: he went in and hung his coat up on the outside of the door, and went in. And old Jay was a little hard of hearing, and he was standing up there, and he waited about a half an hour. And Simon Gunanoot's father's coat was still on the door, and Jay thought he was in there for quite a while. So Jay went down there and opened the door, and the door was vacant. But the coat was there. So they gave the alarm, and by this time, a half an hour had taken place, and Simon's father had got away, and beat it back to Kispiox. He went back to Kispiox then, and then he and Simon, they beat it.

Simon Gunanoot was a man that was very, very well respected. Thought of very highly around there—I knew him personally well, I was with the Hudson Bay Company and we did a lot of business with Simon Gunanoot, and I knew him personally. And when they couldn't get him, Superintendent Hussey, at that time he was the superintendent of pro-vincial police in Victoria, he sent up one of his head men to Hazelton to see what they could do about going out to look for Simon and Peter Himadam. And he got in touch with me. Well, I'd been up in the North Country, up towards Ingineka, the year previous to this, and I knew a little about the country, been in it. So, they asked me if I'd act as a guide in taking out a number of provincial policemen to hunt for Simon. So I was assigned to a man by the name of Wilkie, Otway Wilkie. He was a chief provincial constable in New Westminister. He was sent up, and I went out with him, and we were out, went up around Bear Lake and all through there for about eight or ten months.

Well, Simon had his family; they went north. It was a well-known fact that had it not been for Leclair, the government wouldn't have done any-thing. But Leclair was an innocent man, and that's what the government was out for, to get Simon. As far as McIntosh was concerned, the popular opinion there was that it was coming to McIntosh. McIntosh got mixed up with Simon's wife, and it was deemed then, at that time, that it was coming to McIntosh. While, as far as Leclair was concerned, it was an

Left to right: Chief Constable John Kelly, Simon Gunanoot, Constable Sperry Cline and Inspector Parsons after Gunanoot gave himself up in 1919. Photo: B-04313

innocent man and that's why the government was out to get Simon. But Simon was well respected.

He had an uncle, but— He used to go out and get Pete his fur, bring it in and sell it. Well, I was with the Hudson Bay at that time—we were buying fur. I knew that— we knew that it was Simon's fur, but we didn't see Simon. It was through this uncle of his that we bought the fur, but we, we had an idea that it was Simon's fur. I had been—personally, I was up and bought fur from him, but I wasn't supposed to know it was Simon. I knew him, I knew him before the accident occurred in Hazelton. But we were buying his fur; we never bothered him.

After the government spent about $150,000 for these searches for him, they gave it up and they drifted on. This fellow by the name of Cameron that had the Two Mile House where this fracas occurred, where Gunanoot had shot McIntosh, he disappeared. All the old-timers around there that knew anything about the case had disappeared. Dick

Hamilton, the head of the pack train for the company that he was working with, had died. There were no witnesses.

So when it came to trial, Stuart Henderson came up there with George Beirnes, and they got ahold of Simon, and they went up and interviewed Simon. Well, he didn't want to give himself up. But Stuart Henderson convinced him. But they couldn't do anything with him. The government didn't have a case; they had no witnesses. So finally Simon came in and gave himself up, and they took him down below to New Westminster; he was there for a while, until the trial came on, and when the trial came on, they simply asked for a dismissal. The government had no evidence, all the witnesses had disappeared or died. So, that was the Gunanoot case.

After years afterwards, Simon came to Prince Rupert, and I was walking along the street and this Native stopped me and asked me if I wasn't Bert Glassey, and I said, "Yes." And he said, "Do you remember me?" And I looked at him and I said, "No." I said, "Who are you?" He says, "I'm Simon Gunanoot."

The Country Was Up in Arms

THOMAS BULMAN

on the McLean Gang and the Posse that Followed Them

(RECORDED JUNE 29, 1964)

RANCHER AND historian Thomas Alexander "Alex" Bulman (1911–2000) was born around Kamloops and wrote a popular book called *Kamloops Cattlemen: One Hundred Years Of Trail Dust!*, published in 1972, about the history of the Kamloops ranching business. In it, he argues that most of the integral settlers of early British Columbia were not fur traders or gold miners but the cattlemen who fed them and decided to stay. His father, Joseph Bulman, had come to Canada from England in 1886 and worked on Cherry Creek Ranch as a cattleman and horse trader. The elder Bulman bought the Willow Ranch and kept expanding until, by the time of his death in 1935, he controlled over 40,000 acres. This land was passed on to his two boys, Alex and Joe. Alex had started moving cattle from ranch to ranch for his father at the age of 10.

In this anecdote, Bulman discusses the McLean brothers. Alan, age 25, Charles, 17, and Archie, 15, were the sons of Scottish-born Donald McLean, who was reputed to have a fiery temper. In the wake of the depression of 1877 that hit Kamloops hard, the McLean brothers decided to turn to crime.

On December 3, 1879, the gang stole a stallion from rancher William Palmer, who then reported it to constable and jailer John Ussher. Ussher had little incentive to chase the gang because he knew that they could easily break out of jail at the time. However, when a warrant was

77

Alan McLean, 1880, eldest of the three brothers.
Photo: A-01456/John Batrel Uren

eventually issued promising a huge reward, Ussher, Palmer and a man named John McLeod set out to arrest them. The posse caught up with the gang on December 9, 1879, at their camp near Long Lake near the Douglas Lake Ranch in the Nicola Valley. The outlaws resisted, and both John McLeod and Alan McLean were wounded, and Constable Ussher was killed.

In this story, Bulman mentions several Indians. The people to whom he refers are the Upper Nicola Indian Band, members of the Nicola Tribal Association. They are known in the Okanagan language as the Spaxomin.

·   ·   ·

CD2, TRACK 3

THOMAS BULMAN: The McLeods were two brothers, John and William. When I remember them, I was then just a lad of probably 15, or in my early teens. They were then men getting well on in years. John was a big, tall good-looking man, and a very gaunt-looking fellow, really rugged-looking man. William was a little thicker-set, a little different-looking fellow, and he was the older of the two brothers. They had come, I understand, with the Hudson Bay Company. Now, they ranched, and had good ranches when I remember, out south of here, out in the— well, generally the Barnhartvale into the north end of the Nicola Valley, Campbell Creek area.

It was John McLeod who was one of the posse that attempted to capture the McLean, famous McLean brothers. And I can well remember the bullet marks on John McLeod's face where the musket ball passed through between his jaws—and that left quite a mark on each cheek— and I still remember that as a young boy, knowing the story a bit, you see. He was shot in the leg, also. And I might say, just by way of interest, that where the gunfight took place is on land that I now own. They came upon them there, apparently on a cold early winter day, and this gun battle ensued in which Ussher was immediately shot down and killed, McLeod was badly wounded and Palmer— the musket ball that hit McLeod also passed through his frozen beard, I believe, without any ill effects. So they came back to town and gathered more of a posse. And the fight broke up naturally in favour of the McLean boys, and they immediately broke

Charles McLean after his capture, 1880.
Photo: A-01458/John Batrel Uren

their camp and proceeded towards the direction of the Nicola Country.

Now, they made their way over, first, to Trapp and McDonald's place—there's one of the first lakes out along the highway is called Trapp Lake. The story, as it was told to me by my father, was that they went down to Trapp and McDonald's place, to their little old cabin, with the full intentions of killing them. But they arrived there, and either both of these fellows were pretty good talkers, I guess, and befriended them, and asked them in for something to eat, and just handled them in a such a way that sort of put this killing idea out of their heads for the time being. And they apparently, of course, in the back of their minds, intended to get over to Nicola and get the Nicola Indians to rise in rebellion and drive the whites out of the country. And therefore, they thought, these two men—they weren't old men, they were young men, Trapp and McDonald—but they could get them coming back if they got the Indians to rise in rebellion. Those two men were of no great consequence at that time, so they spared them.

I don't know whether it would be the Douglas Lake Indians or the ones farther down the valley, or just which. And Woodward told me that the massacre of Custer was still fairly fresh in the minds of Indians then. To the extent that they could be roused into thinking that it was possible to wipe the white man out, you understand. And this is what the McLeans had in mind. They thought that they could bring enough pressure on the old chief of the Indians, the Nicola Indians, to get his people in rebellion, because no doubt there was considerable hard feeling and various reasons for them possibly to do that. However, they didn't meet with any success in that line at all. They say the chief of the Nicolas at that time was a very fine man, and a good leader of his people, and knew that it was just complete folly to ever try such a thing. And I guess just didn't, wasn't interested one little bit. So they didn't get any support from the Indians, and consequently were rounded up there in quite short order, when all the whites got out, and got right at the job.

And then they went on from there, and killed Kelly, the sheep herder, just on beyond the McDonald Ranch, a short distance. Now, Kelly was apparently herding this little bunch of sheep for one of the old ranch outfits, and they shot him just in a way of a bet: one of them bet the other he could kill him with the first shot, which he did. And I was told that William McLeod was herding another little bunch of sheep across the valley from that and saw the incident, and of course he got his bunch of sheep out of sight in a hurry, and they didn't ever see him. So that both McLeods were somewhat not exactly involved, but both saw some of their doings.

Then, of course, they went on from there to Douglas Lake, where they were captured. By this time, the whole country was up in arms. They surrounded this cabin at Douglas Lake, near the present Douglas Lake Indian Reserve, and many people, many men, had gathered by this time, and of course, they had them so surrounded that there wasn't a hope of them getting away. They were evidently suffering from thirst, and I guess from hunger, but certainly from thirst because they couldn't get to any water and they'd long since run out of water. I think two or three days elapsed during the siege.

Well, finally, I was told that the posse got a wagonload of hay, dry hay, which they were able to push backwards, and thereby be sheltered from it. And they were able to push it against the shack, or could've done so, and they were close to each other and they yelled to the McLeans that they were going to push this wagonload of hay to the shack and throw a match into it, you see? And the whole thing would've gone up in flames, and they would've had to come out or burn in there.

At only 15, Archie McLean was the youngest of the desperado brothers, 1880.
Photo: A-01459/John Batrel Uren

The cabin at Douglas Lake where the McLeans were captured, ca. 1912.
Photo: A-01457

Whereupon they immediately saw the game was up and yelled that they would give up, and they came out with their hands up. And there was evidently no further— they— there was no further trouble with them. They, I suppose, bound them and took them—I believe they brought them to Kamloops, and then they were taken down over through the canyon to New Westminster, where they were tried and hanged.

And I was told a story not too long ago that John McLeod, who had been wounded, was of course called as a witness, and was still not a very well man when they tried them and it was with quite great difficulty that they got him down to New Westminster as a witness. And as I recall, he had to be, oh, looked after quite carefully; he was still a pretty sick man from these bullet wounds.

I did hear from a man named McQueen, Jim McQueen. He was a friend of the McLeans, I guess, about of their age; he would be the age of the youngest McLean, I think. Because the youngest McLean, who served time in jail, worked for my father as quite an old man. But anyway, McQueen, of course, took their side in the thing. He felt that they hadn't— they'd been wrongly arrested in the first place, that they hadn't stolen this horse, as they were supposed to have done. But of course when I say this, I realized even then that he was biased in their favour, and therefore would accept their story much more readily than he would that of the police. But of course— and maybe it's possible that up until the time of the killing of Ussher, that they might have been— there might have been some truth to this, the fact that they felt they were wrongly arrested. But of course, from the time that they shot and killed Ussher and wounded McLeod, well, they were certainly beyond any hope of anyone taking their side then. They were just simply murderers, and that was all there was to it. And from then on, they were hunted as such.

(4)

Opening Up The West

INFRASTRUCTURE WAS key to growing British Columbia's economy, but it was also essential to managing a burgeoning population. The gold rush had brought north a steady influx of mostly American, mostly "anti-British" prospectors—many of them heavily armed—and Governor James Douglas pleaded with the Colonial Office in London to send help to keep order. The Columbia Detachment of the Royal Engineers, 160 men in all, was sent. Among their duties was to establish a public works program that involved surveying, producing maps and laying out town-sites while helping to build roads and rail lines.

These stories from a railway worker and a surveyor, and an anecdote about one of the earliest mail carriers, detail what life was like opening up an untamed and unknown land while learning to accommodate such unique environments. Their work united various parts of the province and the people who lived there. And they made it possible for doctors and ministers and teachers to venture far inland and far north, bringing many immigrants into contact with small First Nations communities for the first time.

FACING: *A survey camp, ca. 1900. Photo: A-00812*

Beyond the Next Hill

FORIN CAMPBELL

on the Life of a Surveyor in British Columbia

(RECORDED JULY 19, 1964)

JOHN ALEXANDER Forin Campbell (1887–1982) was among the first non-Native people to be based in Fort George, later the city of Prince George, in 1908. He first moved west from Collingwood, Ontario, where he was born, to join his father, Rev. John Campbell, Sr., who had been appointed as the pastor of the First Presbyterian Church in Victoria in 1892. Known as Forin or "Doc" to friends and family, the younger Campbell completed his schooling in Victoria, then moved to Prince George to work on a survey gang, Gore and McGregor. Each surveyor earned $75 a month plus board and was expected to work six days a week from five in the morning until five at night.

Campbell was among the first surveyors in northern BC and his work helped create detailed maps of the territory that were instrumental in settling the area from Fort St. James to Quesnel, and from McBride to Burns Lake. These are huge expanses that now contain many towns and communities. Besides making maps, Campbell was a student of the history of the North and while travelling he retraced the routes of early explorers such as Simon Fraser. He learned much of the land by asking questions from the First Nations people he met and, later in life, was in demand as a speaker. He could substantiate his claims such as "Fort St. James was the first capital of BC where the first white settlement was made, and it had the first farm in BC," with stories from his own experience.

FACING: *Survey work near Great Slave Lake. Early surveyors tramped across the whole of northern BC, never knowing what lay beyond the next hill. Photo: c-06526*

87

This interview provides rare insight into the methodology, lifestyle and travel of a surveyor opening up the west, and how many hours and how much commitment he put into his craft.

．　　　．　　　．

CD2, TRACK 4 FORIN CAMPBELL: I first came into this country I was a schoolboy in Victoria; and like all schoolboys—this was 1908—I wanted to get a job and we went down to the survey office and—and when I arrived here in May 1908, the population of what you call Prince George—it was then called Fort George—were three: three white men. That was the permanent population. There was the Hudson's Bay man, [James] Cowie. There was a man by the name of A.G. Hamilton, who was an ex–North-West Mounted Police man, and he was what you called a free trader. And he had a little place on the riverbank and he had a certain advantage over the Hudson Bay. The Hudson Bay did not sell any whiskey; they had to

A dog team outside the Hudson's Bay store in Fort George where James Cowie worked, ca. 1880. Photo: B-00338

get their whiskey from Quesnel. And he would make whiskey; he would take tobacco juice and cayenne pepper and Worcestershire sauce and water and mix it up and sell it to the Indians at two-and-a-half a bottle, and the Indians were having a fine time. That's how he'd buy his furs from them, and the Indians would say, "Well, we is just like a white man. It makes us sick just like a white man!" And the other man was a man that lived just across the Nechako River by the name of Capee and he was killed in the war. And that was the total population in 1908.

And, of course, we had to come in by pack train; there were no trails. And in winter, of course, we travelled by canoes—or in summer by canoes and in winter, of course, we travelled by dog team. And dog team travel is probably the hardest travelling going. We'd have about six dogs and we'd start from here to go north and—up to the Finlay River and away north through the—as far as the Yukon in fact, we went with our dog teams. And we had to carry feed for the dogs, naturally, that was the main thing, and the main thing was rice for the dogs. And each man was allowed on the party thirty pounds. And I remember one man, he had served in the Royal Marines, he got to Quesnel and he was quite a drinker and he wanted to take whiskey along. The chief of the party said, "That's all right, as long as you do not exceed thirty pounds." So he took a case of whiskey from Quesnel and threw away some of his blankets. And I remember the first night on the trail it was about thirty below zero and he broke open this case from the toboggan and then we all took a drink. The next morning we couldn't eat and then we realized we're drinking whiskey at thirty below zero and we had frozen our throats. And that's one thing we learned—never to drink whiskey at thirty below unless you mix water with it.

And at night, of course, we wouldn't carry any tents on our dog teams, and it was just a fly. And the first thing we'd do is clear the snow away because if we pitched our camp on top of the snow we'd gradually sink down. And the men would get wood. We'd have to stop at a place that had plenty of wood and cut the timber down about eight feet in length and build it up in front. And then, of course, we had this fly, and as long as your fire was burning you will be quite warm, even at forty below; but if the fire went down, we'd get cold. And then, of course—to go north, of course, it was all poling on the river and we start from Quesnel. There were no boats at that time on the river, and we'd have to pole up to Quesnel to a place north of here about thirty miles and we'd take our canoes and we'd portage them across to the headwaters of the Arctic Slope to Summit Lake, that's about eight miles. And we'd have to take our canoes across on rollers. Of course, the banks there would be two or three hundred feet high, we'd have to pull these enormous forty-foot canoes up there—take them across the eight miles and then back and forth and we'd carry the grub across and go north. And then we'd reverse the process when we came back in the fall of the year. But that was the surveying in the early days, you know.

Yes, of course, our main thing would be bacon and beans. That's about all we'd carry and then live on the country with fish and all the rest.

IMBERT ORCHARD: And game too.

CAMPBELL: And game.

And those were the surveyors of the country, mapping the country; there were no maps of the country—just finding what was in the country. And we travelled in the Finlay River and all the rivers to the north and all over the country. No planes, of course, we just had to go by foot, backpack or use horses where there were trails or river canoes when there were rivers.

We were covering, well, the whole of northern British Columbia; pretty well north of the CPR track right up to the northern boundary. You know, you had to get over and just find what's beyond the next hill. No one knew at the time, and we put that on the map, and they'd get it in Victoria and from that they would make the maps of the country. That's the first maps made outside of rough maps made by Father Maurice and the CPR and those who came through here first. And Mackenzie and Simon Fraser, of course.

Well, our headquarters were in South Ford and Fort George, see that's at the Hudson Bay post. Our real headquarters were in Victoria, of course. We'd go from there. And we'd use Indians entirely except a few white men for the instrument men. Well, the Indians, it seemed—the

Poling up the river was the only way to travel north from Quesnel, 1920.
Photo: 1-58495/Frank Cyril Swannel

Indians don't know what's beyond; the Indians are very localized. They know their country right around, but you get them fifty or sixty miles away, they're lost just like a white man. They don't know the country.

But in those days we'd go along the trails or the rivers and we'd be backpacking with horses or with canoes and we'd want to cache some of our grub or some of our equipment, we'd put it by the side of the trail or by the side of the river up in a tree with a little— to protect it from the bears. And we put some tin around it to stop the bears from climbing. We'd come back the next day, the next week or the next year and that stuff would still be there. The Indians or— no one else would touch that grub. And any cache in those days was sacred; well, you cannot do that now. We'd leave our rifles, ammunition, it would all be there.

And the same way, all the cabins in the country, they would never lock a cabin door. Now the reason of that is, suppose a man in the depth of winter, we'll say thirty or forty below, and he had broken through the ice somewhere and frozen— and wet as wheat; well, he had to get to a cabin or where there's a fire to thaw out again and he might know there's a cabin a mile away. If he got to that cabin and the door was locked, well, that would be end of him; he couldn't get in. And in each cabin there was always dry wood and all a man had to do was to go in that cabin, start a fire and thaw out. There'd be grub there. And when he left all he had to do was replace the dry wood so the next man coming along would get it. Now that's the way the old-timers were, but you can't do that now.

The only thing is, if it got forty below zero, we weren't supposed to go out from the camp; it was too cold, not for ourselves but for the dogs. But we didn't carry a thermometer, we'd just have to guess when it's forty-five below.

It's a permanent job; you just kept moving all over the country, yet it wouldn't get monotonous because you were never in one place very long. You'd be a few days in one camp and then you'd pack up and move on to another camp. And as I say, it was all of that "beyond the next hill," "what's beyond that range of mountains?"

And on a triangulation of course now they use the helicopters; they can get up there, the surveyors. In those days we had to backpack to

By 1910, two years after Forin Campbell first arrived, South Fort George had grown.
Photo: B-00344

every mountaintop. Now, I backpacked to the top of mountains from Bella Coola right to the northern end of the province there. Walking in with the men and back; we'd see a mountain, we'd climb to the top and put our triangulation in there and go to the next mountain, read the angles and so on. It was all packing. And then we would just, as I said, see what's beyond the next range. And we'd climb to a top of a mountain and we'd see another mountain. We'd take our angles and we'd go to that mountain and so on and we'd keep on going.

When I first came—well, of course, this country was at one time a very heavily timbered country and in the 1860s—in '62 and '63 when the money around Barkerville—to clear the timber and get down so they could mine, they started fires down there. Well, the old Indians told me, I think it was in 1860 or— '61 or '62, a fire started in the Quesnel area, swept up through here, swept across the Vanderhoof area and then it smoldered all the winter under the snow and the next year it started up again. And that Vanderhoof area, especially, was almost a prairie land when I saw it. You could drive across it with a four-horse team almost anywhere, and all those trees that you see there are all—except in a few clumps—are all less than 60 years old.

Then, of course, being heavily timbered there was no such thing as moose here. The moose didn't come into this country until about, oh, sixty years ago, and then they started drifting in as the heavy timber disappeared. There was no pasture for them, and as the country opened up the moose came in and the deer also.

It's not a very exciting life. You'd leave your headquarters—usually my headquarters in Victoria—we'd come up here— if we didn't stay all winter we'd come up in the fall or in the spring and start in on our work and we'd just keep on plugging away until that particular work was finished. Then we'd go back and make up our plans and make up our notes and turn them in to the government and then start off the next year. It's not a very exciting life. It's a hard life. When the weather's poor you couldn't do anything; now I've been sometimes on the top of a mountain or something. We'd just be held there—I have been held as long as ten days; you couldn't do a thing. Though the only hazards are breaking a leg, or cutting yourself with an axe or getting drowned, of course, in a river if you're not careful. And yes— we can always get across a river; we can swim the horses or if you can't get across like that we can build a raft. And we can always push the raft off and some distance downstream we'd get to the other shore. But we'd no trouble crossing a river; or you could even build a rough canoe, you know, it takes a few days to do that— a dugout canoe. But you're never in a hurry—well, you can't be in a hurry. And you don't rush but you work long hours: ten or twelve hours a day would be our day's work.

We'd have a rifle in camp. We'd never carry a rifle outside because we'd already be laden down, men with axes and our instruments. No, we'd never carry rifles, wouldn't carry revolvers or anything else; except as I said, one rifle in camp maybe for going out hunting game.

Those Hudson Bay men, they were all for the company. I can remember years ago in Fort McLeod—that's the first white settlement in British Columbia west of the Rocky Mountains, 1806 it was established—and years ago I was coming out of the country from the north and we're out of grub and we're living on fish. And I was telling the men, I had about twelve men with me, "It will be all right when we arrive at Fort McLeod, there's lots of grub there." So we got to Fort McLeod and I camped across the river. I went across to see the Hudson Bay man and I told him what I wanted and he started to make up the list of stuff. He said, "I don't like to sell this to you," he said, "Anyone coming into the country." The Hudson Bay didn't want white men coming in then. Well, I said, "I'm not coming in, I'm going out." "Oh," he said, "That's all right then." And he made out the list. Then I pulled my chequebook out. It's a chequebook on the government trust account; that's how surveyors—they always carry this— their own chequebook on the government trust—and I was going to write. "No," he said, "I don't accept any cheques." But I said, "Tommy, this is a government cheque." He said, "I don't care," he said, "Our orders are to take no cheques. I won't take any cheques, but however," he said, "I'll tell you what I'll do." He said, "I'll pay for it," and he said, "You can send me the money back." And he said— he went over to the safe and he opened it up and he said, "This is $50 of my own money." And he took his own money and put it into the Hudson Bay till and he said, "When you get out," he said, "The first man coming down next year"— this was in the fall, no one would be coming down in winter— He said, "You send the $50 down." "Well," I said, "I might never send it down." And he said, "Oh, I'll take a chance on that," but he said, "I won't give you credit but," he said "I'll pay for the grub myself."

Now that's typical of a Hudson Bay man. They were all for the company. And Tommy retired; Tommy worked with them sixty-two years and he started when he was 15, and he got a pension of $50 a month. And he was in his— well, on his seventies when he quit. That was the Hudson Bay. But they were very honest, all those Hudson Bay men, and all for the company.

.   .   .

When Forin Campbell resupplied in Fort McLeod, the Hudson's Bay man wouldn't give him credit but instead lent him $50 of his own money, 1906. Photo: A-04271

In 1914, Campbell enlisted in the Royal Canadian Engineers where he served in France with the 48th Battalion. His two brothers, Gordon and "Rusty," were also sent to the front, as was their father who was a pastor for the 50th Gordon Highlanders. Campbell was promoted to the rank of major in 1917 and was decorated with the Military Cross and the Croix de Guerre. In 1918 he was charged with commanding the Royal Canadian Engineers group in Siberia, and over the six months he was there he became one of the first Canadians to fight Communists.

After the war, Campbell returned to Prince George where he married Mary Elizabeth (Bertha) Skinner in 1922. When the Labour Department was formed in the 1930s, he was hired as an inspector and was responsible for enforcing BC's labour laws throughout the area north of the C.N.R. line to Prince Rupert.

When World War II broke out, Campbell became the district engineer for Military District Number 13. Among other duties, he was charged with setting up bases from Edmonton through the Arctic to Fort Churchill for Operation Muskox. Many were located in places where humans had never gone before, and he flew for days on end organizing his patrols to carry supplies and dropping goods out of the planes for his team. The operation was completed on time and also achieved its goal of supplying the caravan of military vehicles with more than 300,000 gallons of gasoline.

The Ties Keep On Coming

DAVID ROSS

on Building the Railroad from Prince Rupert

(DATE OF RECORDING UNKNOWN)

FOR YEARS, the boundary between the Yukon and Alaska was never clearly defined. By the time the gold rush was in full swing in the Klondike, Canada was pushing for a clear resolution on the issue, hoping that it would include a direct route entirely through Canada to the sea. However, in 1903, arbiters decided to uphold the present boundaries, and Prime Minister Laurier decided that a port would be needed on the west coast of Canada in order to compete with the Americans. Prince Rupert was chosen as that terminal. To connect Prince Rupert with the rest of Canada, the Grand Trunk Pacific Railway, a 4,800-kilometre line from Winnipeg to Prince Rupert, was built between 1906 and 1914. In this interview, David Ross (b. 1890) describes what it was like to work on the railway.

Born on a farm in Sutherland in northern Scotland, Ross came to Canada as an 18-year-old in search of his own farm and job opportunities. He found work on the prairies for $30 a month, working on ranches. By 1911, Ross heard the buzz about Prince Rupert and moved west to help construct the railway. He offers invaluable insight into life on the remote coast of British Columbia.

·   ·   ·

DAVID ROSS: Well, when they were— when they were putting the Grand Trunk Pacific through this country, like up through the Skeena Valley

CD2, TRACK 5

and the Bulkley Valley, lots of people wondered why they were building a railroad in there. There was no people in the country that time. Very, very few anyway, maybe a few government linemen. That's about who it was had the government telegraph lines through. Well, it opened up the country. That's what it was for. A lot of people figured the Bulkley Valley was a good farming country and it proved to be that way. And the same around Smithers and Hazelton. They had river boats on— you know, coming up the Skeena River from Prince Rupert up to Hazelton. But when they were building the railroad, they thought it was— even after it was completed, after it joined up, I wonder what they built a railroad through this country for. [laughs]

Come out in 1908. Oh, there was a lot of young fellows leaving the north of Scotland. They thought Canada was a good place to go to, and there was lots of land to be had for $10 for 160 acres. And there was supposed to be lots of work. Wages wasn't very big, but I went to work on a farm for $30 a month and my board, when I come out, thirty miles south of Medicine Hat. I come to Medicine Hat first. And then, oh 1911, we heard all about this booming place of Prince Rupert. So I thought I'd take my chances and go up there and see if I could get on the railway. And that's what I did.

No, there wasn't much there. Oh, there was— there was a theatre and three or four hotels and a lot of men down there. There was a lot of construction men. And the city was trying to make streets through the rocks and muskeg down there. Everything was done by hand, horses and, and men, and blasting, yes blasting. Labourers were paid the big sum of 30¢ an hour. [laughs] And the first job I had was tamping ties, making a railroad yard in Prince Rupert in what they called Prince Rupert Yard. That's the first job I had. And then I went on in the spring of 1912 I went up the country with the steam shovels and the likes of that and hung out on them. Nineteen thirteen I got on the— I was hired as a brake man. So I— and I stayed with that ever since. I kept on going with the railroad, extended every year until it joined up at Fort Fraser in 19, April 1914. And this is when I come in to Prince George, after they joined up. Crew, steel crew working from the east end, and a steel— and the Prince Rupert crew working from the west end.

Blasting at Prince Rupert, April 1913, to clear the ground for the new Grand Trunk Pacific Railway line from Prince Rupert to Winnipeg. Photo: A-00456/McRae Brothers

First of all, the grade had to be built. And that was all done with— out of Prince Rupert that was all— nearly all blasting for miles, blasting that was built through rocks. But when they got farther inland, then it was a case of horses and scrapers and no such thing as bulldozers then. This was just horses and scrapers and lots of men and their picks and shovels making the grade. Well, after the grade is built, they put the track layer on there. Track was mostly— the track laying was mostly laid in the fall. And as soon as spring come, like in April, they built with the ballast trains ballasting. Maybe there was fifty miles of track to ballast. They do that all in the summer, start as soon as the— soon as bright in the morning. As soon as you could see to load gravel and unload it, work fifteen, sixteen hours a day, just going all the time, not one train, but three or four.

IMBERT ORCHARD: Now, could you describe a pioneer to me in some detail? What was it?

ROSS: Well, it's a machine. It's just like a kind of a derrick to handle the rails, instead of manhandling them. There's a carload of rails right behind it, next car to it. And they get a hold of these rails and keep them going on up the front, one on each side of the track. This goes on all the time. And the ties come up on a tram.

ORCHARD: This changes—

ROSS: This is an endless thing. It goes, keeps on going. It's in a kind of a trough and the ties keep on coming up. And there's a crew behind that, and as soon as one car is empty, they take it out of there and switch it out and put on another one. There was always a material train, what they call the material, with their material, whatever they wanted. There'd be a train with boxes of spikes on it, and bolts. And one with— a car with spikes and bolts, another one with— two or three with ties and two or three with rails. The crew on that, and they had to keep them supplied. And you had to keep moving so that there wouldn't be too much gravel

Building a bridge for the Grand Trunk Pacific Railway at Prince George, 1913.
Photo: D-00499

in one place and get underneath the wheel and get derailed. This took a lot of time to get the car back on. And of course, there was always a gang of trackmen there to put the ballast under the ties. Lift the rail up. Lift the ties up. Poke it in there.

Well, they had engineers there. They had engineers. And when you laid a mile of rails, engineers come there and give you the proper centres. And they put a little wooden pin in the centre and a tack in it. And when the men

Construction of the Grand Trunk Pacific Railway, 1913. This enormous construction project involved a lot of heavy labour done by hand. Labourers were paid 30¢ an hour.
Photo: B-00319

would come through with their bars, they lined it up by hand. And every now and again, they'd put their tape on and measure from this little tack and the pin to the inside of the rail. And if that was the certain distance, if that was right, that was the way it was. And they lined up from that. When them fellows got through with that, I wouldn't like to stand at one end and fellow fire a rifle at me, because it was really straight—

ORCHARD: Yes, I see.

ROSS: —the way they did it. When they put that grade out of Prince Rupert, that was very solid, because it was all nearly rock bottom. And I seen them trains making sixty miles an hour there, with the first shot of ballast. Because it was all solid on the bottom, it's just rock.

There's stations. There's— the Grand Trunk Pacific had stations about every six miles. There was Terrace and Amsbury and then Shames and Exstew, Salvus, Kwinitsa, Skeena City, and Tyee, Sockeye. There was no Port Edward them days. Phelan and then Kaien, that's the first station out of Rupert. There was no— there was never a station there, just a shack. But that was six miles out of Kaien. These stations were used for the section crews to stay in. Section men, they all had— there would be a foreman and three or four men on every six miles of track.

I don't know. It was all— They were all— belonged to the contractors to follow as the steward. And they brought up all the supply. They brought up horses. They brought up cattle. They brought up everything: oats, feed, hay, feed for the horses, feed for the men. The cattle was brought up live and they were slaughtered along the— where they could— as near as they could get to the construction work. They had butchers there slaughtered their own cattle. Then they were taken up through the country to their— with four-horse teams. Had a big slaughterhouse at Hazelton. And they used the tote roads. I'd see them killing the cattle there, and then they were shipped out with a four-horse teams. I don't know what they did— how long that meat would keep because in the summer it was pretty hot.

The Grand Trunk Pacific Railway at Pacific Station, 1914. Photo: D-04077

From Daylight to Dark

MARTIN STARRET

on Billy Bristol and Running Mail up the Fraser Canyon

(RECORDED MARCH 24, 1963)

MARTIN STEVENS Starret (1888–1973) was a gifted storyteller and an exceptional resource for anecdotes from the Babine region all the way down to Hope. He had learned to speak Chinook and took a genuine interest in learning about the land from people he met and befriended. Of the 998 people that Imbert Orchard interviewed, his favourite was Starret, and the two recorded more than twenty hours of tape together.

Starret is clearly one of our province's most interesting and important raconteurs, in part because his stories include a wide range of characters. In *Voices of British Columbia,* the first book in this series, he recounted stories about train robber Bill Miner and mule packer Cataline. In this book, he recalls mail carrier Bill Bristol, a pioneer that the history books have long since forgotten. In his narrative, Starret paints a vivid picture of the Crown Colony of British Columbia (still part of British North America) around the very first gold rush in 1858 when the non-Native population jumped from around 200 people to somewhere around 30,000. This was still thirty years before the railway came into British Columbia, so people were still travelling by steamships, canoes and pack trains. None of the technologies and infrastructures that we now take for granted were in place, so the mail was the main means of communication in a province full of remote communities. Starret captures what it would have been like for men like Bristol who had no experience travelling in the rugged environments.

.   .   .

"Red Shirt Bill" Bristol, mail carrier from Westminster to Yale, ca. 1880.
Though unused to travelling in rugged environments, Bristol was a man of great
endurance, or "stay-with-it-y." Photo: A-02022

MARTIN STARRET: He is known as Bill Bristol. Where he acquired that name, I don't know. He said he's been called "'Red Shirt Bill,' 'Magpie Bill,' but it was always Bill anyway, so I got the name— been called by the name of Bill Bristol."

Mr. Bristol was in this country before my father; he came here in 1858. There was only one man in my time who had been to this country before Mr. Bristol, and that was old Dad Yates at the Hudson's Bay Company, who came in 1855. He must've come over the trail the same year, and maybe just after or just before, when Simon Fraser's son was buried out here on Manson Mountain, it's supposed to be about fifteen miles out of town. It was the same year, 1855. And this Bill Bristol, he was born in Syracuse, New York, and he'd come around the Horn in a windjammer, and he got off at San Francisco, or 'Frisco, as he used to call it. And he worked in the mines there, in the— '49, 1849. And he must've hung around there quite a while, because he came up here in 1858. And as far as I know, he didn't get any farther than, I guess it was Sailor Bar or American Bar above Hope here. And then, I understand—now this is not clear to me altogether, but I understand that this river transportation—these river transportation people, old William Irving, or a young man, Captain John Irving, by their influence somehow or other, Mr. Bristol became possessor of 200 acres of land, 200-acre block of timberland. And this was a Dominion grant. And he had that for the purpose of supplying— of cutting the timber—the fir timber for wood of the steamboats. And that landing was just at the foot of where the international booming ground is now, and it was known as Bristol's Landing. As I said before, I think he got a dollar and a quarter a cord for his wood piled up on the bank.

Mr. Bristol, I dare say, from 1865 on until 1885, he got the job from the Barnard's Express Company for carrying mail and express between Westminster and Yale. And when the weather was good in the early fall, when it was too shallow for the boats to come up, why, he'd use a rowboat. Only in the season when the boats couldn't run, of course, when the water was shallow, like in the fall and early spring. All winter, too, of course. And then, when the winter came, he'd use nothing but a dugout cedar canoe with shovelnose to go over the ice. There was ice running in the water, icebergs. I suppose some of them would be ten feet across, and some of them only three or four feet across. Maybe some of them would be twenty feet across, and the ice may be six inches to a foot thick. Well, he'd go in on these, and he'd get the old canoe on top of some of them, and then he'd back up and get in between them and push around with poles and paddles and get by that way. And he had to line it outside with tin, it was lined with sheet metal or tin, so the ice wouldn't cut the canoe. I remember him telling me this over and over again.

He employed nothing but an Indian crew to work with him, as he could, I suppose, perhaps not exactly bully them, but encourage them to a greater extent than he could his— or, white people that he might employ. And another thing, an Indian wasn't afraid to jump out into the water and wade. And if it was shallow, he didn't object to getting his feet wet, as he was brought up that way, catching salmon, etc. So, he preferred an Indian crew to any white man he could hire. In fact, there were very few white men who had been born in the country at that time. And stepping out of the canoe after it was landed would never let go of the paddle, he'd carry it uptown with this mail sack or two on one shoulder, and the paddle. And he said the paddle, he'd have it as protection against the Indian dogs that had come to bite him, he looked so queer in this red shirt and hunched over these mail sacks, that they all wanted to bark at him, because being an unusual sight coming up the beach. And then he would go to the post office and get the mail. And where the express came from, I don't know, I suppose there was an express office in Westminster at that time, and he'd carry express too on the river. Now, what the prices were and what salary he got, I'm unable to tell you. I never heard that.

He'd carried his mail through thick and thin with an Indian crew, and hours, those days when

Steamboat captain John Irving, founder of the John Irving Navigation Company, ca. 1885. Photo: A-01740/ I. W. Taber

F.S. Barnard in the doorway of the Barnard Express Company office in Victoria,
1870s. Photo: A-05939/Maynard (?)

it was from daylight until dark, and sometimes it was dark most of the
time, especially in the winter. Because he always got that mail there
pretty nearly on time. Very seldom he was late getting that mail through
the Yale, or down the other way to Westminster.

IMBERT ORCHARD: What kind of a character was he?

STARRET: Well, he was a very loud mouth, and he would profane. I know
a lot of these profane men that are whirlwinds, and he was one. And he
was not exceptionally good at anything, but it was his remarkable way of
stay-with-it-y, I guess you would call it. For instance, in after years, he
walked from Princeton right over to Hope in a day. He was a man about
five-feet-nine, well chested, barrel chest on him. Very, very strongly built.
But as I say, there was nothing exceptional about what he could do as far

as his strength was concerned, it was the stamina that counted with him, the stay-with-it-y.

He didn't care what people thought of him, that was the least of his trouble; he never worried what people thought of him. What he wanted was results when working, or something like that. And that's the way he was, he seldom got tired, but of course, I guess he would sleep quite a lot at that. And he died in the winter of 1909. Now, that's the end of Mr. Bristol as far as I know.

And Everyone Was Curious

VERA BASHAM

on Teaching the Nisga'a in Their Own Community

(RECORDED NOVEMBER 9, 1965)

VERA ADELINE Basham (née Chasteney, b. 1895) was born in Winnipeg. Research has yielded little about her, and if it were not for Orchard recording her, she would be lost to history. In fact, her story is among the most important in the Orchard Collection. She was among the countless women who contributed tremendously toward improving the lives of the people whom she contacted: in her case, to educating and empowering an entire community to whom she was a foreigner.

Vera was born to Harriett and Alfred Gunson Chasteney, who came to Winnipeg from Great Yarmouth, Norfolk, England in 1889. Alfred Chasteney worked as a clerk while in Winnipeg. We also know that she had two older siblings, George and Rosalie, and a younger sister named Kathleen. Her family moved to Vancouver in 1907, and Basham later enrolled in the Provincial Normal School to get her teacher training. From 1901 to 1956, the school was publicly funded by the Department of Education.

A significant part of Basham's story details her journey up the Nass River to the First Nations community where she was to teach, in 1915. Much has been written about how residential schools had very negative impacts on Native communities and stigmatized or destroyed many cultural practices in all areas of British Columbia. This is not that story. Basham travelled to the community of Aẏans (the original Aiyansh), three miles below the community of Gitla<u>x</u>t'aamiks, which is about 100 kilometres north of Terrace. It is one of four Nisga'a villages, and the capital of the Nisga'a Nation. She taught in the chief's house; in fact, Chief Timothy Derrick (K'eexkw) lived in a smaller room off the side of the house so that the main room could be used for schooling. And though the federal government funded this school, it was a day school attended by the children in the community. The students lived at home with their families, and the only outsiders allowed permanently in the community were the two teachers.

Chief Derrick's house was often described as "being like a hotel" and featured a wraparound verandah. The home was huge by Nisga'a standards, and during the time that he served as chief councillor for Aẏans, it was commonly used to shelter out-of-town guests or government officials. In this story, it is clear that the visitors respected the community atmosphere and value system promoted by Chief Derrick. The people of Aẏans relocated to the village of Gitlaxt'aamiks after the 1917 flood.

. . .

CD2, TRACK 7 VERA BASHAM: My family right through were all teachers. I had only one aim in life, and that was to become a teacher, from the time I was a very small child. So, I continued my education in Vancouver. When I graduated from Normal, I set about to find a position. It was very hard at first, but eventually I saw an advertisement in the paper and was told that if I had a friend to come with me, there was a position for two of us way up in the wilds of the north, that was all I knew about the place. So I took my friend, and in all, there were three teachers and two nurses appointed to go to the north, the Nass River. The nurses were to teach hygiene in the village, and to be housekeepers for the teachers. We didn't live together; we were mostly separated. We dropped these others off along the way. And we had three days' notice to get ready and to order a year's supply of groceries.

It called for speed. And finally we embarked, we went north on the old union steamship *Chelohsin*. As far as Prince Rupert. There, we were taken off, given a rest, and a few days later, we carried on to the port of Mill Bay, under the escort of a Royal North-West Mountie. At Mill Bay, we camped the night in an empty cabin, the five women and the Mountie

The 1901 graduating class of the Provincial Normal School in Vancouver, where Vera Basham was later trained as a teacher. Photo: D-02605

somewhere, and the nurses, the matrons made baked biscuits, and made sandwiches for the trip up the river. This, Mill Bay, was the point of the river on which we embarked to go inland. Seventy-five miles, our trip would be, up the river. And we landed at Mill Bay about four-thirty in the afternoon, in November, this was. It was getting dark, and Indians crowded around to take a look, and see what these people were like that were coming up to teach them, and we got into this cabin, and we put ourselves up for the night. We slept on the floor, I remember, with all our clothes on.

I think it was a cannery, really, but where we were, it was a tiny little store, such a country store would have just chocolate bars, a few things, you know. And a cabin or two, I think of the Indians, I think of the Indian people, because they come down to the canneries in the summertime. In the next morning, we were supposed to be up, we were up at five o'clock in the morning, the Indians had to make an early start to get going. We had seventy-five miles to go up the river in a small gasoline boat. This boat had its engine in the undercover, the rest was a tarpaulin cockpit, and that small space contained the five ladies, the big Mountie, the Indian engineer and helper, and a huge dog that friends had given us in Prince Rupert called Mutt. And all of us sat crowded in that small space: if one was tired and wanted to move, everybody had to move.

So, we were told to get up at five in the morning to start out early. We were up, we were ready to go; no Indians appeared. They didn't come on the scene until eleven o'clock that morning, so we finally embarked. I remember being handed down a ladder from the wharf; it was low tide, the boat was far below. This ladder was so coated with ice that we had to be handed down this thing into the boat, and finally, crossed Mill Bay, very rough. Twice I thought we would capsize, caught in the trough of the waves, but we crossed the bay successfully and went on our way. The interesting thing that day was to see otters swimming in the river, and hundreds of bald-headed eagles perched on the leafless trees. This was so late in the year, you know, it was very bleak looking. Uneventful. And we pulled into Laxgalts'ap, it's now called Greenville, it was an Indian village. And there had been two teachers there from England for quite some few years; they had done very good work. We went and were received into their home, they gave us a nice hot meal, and we had to talk, of course, told them what was happening in the outside world, you know, there were no radio— there was no radio in those days. And we were put up again on the floor that night, all fully clothed. [laughs] And set out the next morning, the same thing happened, we were to make an early start, but the Indians didn't appear, so we got on our way about ten-thirty, something like that.

The next day, we were travelling in this northeasterly direction, the river was low, and the mountains seemed to encroach on us ever closer as we went along. The river became so shallow that the boat had difficulty in making its way up. This boat was the last boat of the season, and after that it would have to be dog team. So, the boat reached the shallows, and an Indian boy of 18, a husky lad, climbed overboard at the shore, and we climbed on his back one by one, with our arms around his neck, holding very tightly, and he took us ashore, and dumped us into, well, snow about up to our knees. And we would walk quite some distance through this snow, while the Indians pulled the boat along the shore. This happened about four times the first day—this would be the second day—and several times the next day. And each time he would have to pack six of us ashore and then bring us back to the boat. Never a complaint, very sure-footed man. And that is how we came through the second day.

We didn't know what we were going up to, and so we were not very well equipped. I remember I had heavy shoes, and I had the old-fashioned spats with the buttons down the side, you know? Up to the knee and down. So we weren't at all equipped. I think the others, some of them had rubbers and that sort of thing. And the last time that we were brought— carried back onto the boat, we were getting awfully tired by this time, it was getting late in the afternoon, one of the housekeepers, or one of the nurses I should say, slipped, and went from one side of the boat right over and fell off into forty feet of water. But fortunately, she managed to seize hold of the rail as she went over, and clung to it. So, they pulled the poor lady up, and the water was icy. And we got her to shed a few of her clothes, and we wrapped her in a blanket that was available and she sat there shivering, and the boat took its way along. And after a half an hour, suddenly the vessel stopped. And when they went to find out what was the cause of it, the blanket was revolving around the crankshaft, the propeller shaft, and it had gradually dragged until it had stopped the motor.

Well, they untangled that, and after a short while we landed at Gwinaha, a pretty little village called Gwinaha. With just, oh, I think about, maybe twelve houses, twelve families in it. And this was where we were to drop one nurse and one teacher. All the Indians came down to the shore to welcome us. And as we got off the boat, here was this poor nurse wrapped in a blanket, you know. The rest of the party left these two ladies there, and we continued on.

Now after we left the little place of Gwinaha, there's a canyon there,

A boat landing on the banks of Aýans, 1890s. Photo: B-07638

and it's very difficult for boats to get through, especially at shallow water. So we were put ashore again, and we walked over lava beds, a terrific amount of lava there. Trackless sort of place. And they pulled the boat through somehow, and we got on to the upper reaches. And from there on, we had many times to be carried to shore, and so on, a repetition of yesterday. Finally, we were met about four-thirty, five, by the whole of this village of Aýans. They all came down to the river, and they all leant willing hands to help unload what we had in the way of hand baggage. Our other stuff was coming on another boat. And there was a brass band there, and they played the band. And all of us proceeded up the village main street to the little house that we were to have, and everyone was so helpful. And everyone was so curious, you know.

So, we went into this home, this little house had been a hotel, or a stopping place you might say, for people going through in the gold rush days, and now it was turned over for our use. We paid rent, a little rent for it, and it was a nice little place but not built very well for the winter, for the climate. And we went in there, and I think the happiest sight I have ever seen was a boiling kettle on the stove singing merrily, and all together we were made to feel quite welcome. The owners of this place, Indians, of course, had laid a table with a white cloth and some silverware of all things. And it was an effort to make us welcome. Our supplies, our trunks and our groceries—a tremendous amount of groceries, they told us that we had nearly a ton between us—came up on another boat, just after, just following us. And that boat struck a snag in the river, and everything but the sugar and the flour became soaked, sodden. However, I never did quite understand how the sugar was kept dry. However, be that as it may, everything was wet. And they brought our trunks in and put them in the hall. We unlocked them so that we would be able to get to them quickly for anything we wanted. And then busied ourselves in the kitchen about getting the evening meal.

Somebody wanted an apron out of one of these trunks, and I went into the hall to get it. And there, I saw three or four Indian men had gone through these trunks. They'd come in silently in moccasin feet—in the front door, while we were busy in the back of the house—and they had gone into the trunks and they had taken out dresses, and held them up, you know, and had put them on. And they were having the most delightful chuckle about this sort of thing. [laughs] So, of course, we called the policeman again, and he soon had them out of the clothes and out of the house, and after that we kept the front door locked because we didn't wish to have silent visitors coming in [laughs].

About the supplies, for weeks and weeks, we had tea and raisins and dates, and such things as that, spread out on pieces of cheesecloth around the kitchen stove on the floor drying. We, fortunately, had taken up a whole bolt of cheesecloth to use for possibly curtains or tablecloths or anything—we didn't know what we were going to. And so we cut squares of this and put the tea drying there. As soon as one batch dried, we gathered it up into a bag and tied it and hung it away, and you can imagine how nice our tea tasted all the year. Why, we lived on that.

I should say here that there had been, in this village, a missionary from Britain. He'd been there quite some years, and he had done wonderful work with the Indians, but he had not taught them English. He had learned their language right from the beginning, and he had even made an alphabet and given them some sort of a printing—had a little printing press set up. They had one or two little primers in their own language, but it was a great drawback when we went up, they had—they couldn't speak English. The chief, and just one or two of the others understood a little. I think Chief's English was perhaps better than any. And so, that put us in a very hard position, coming right out of Normal, and having classes, and having none of the language.

And so, each evening for weeks, we had this boy Felix that had packed us in and out of the boat on the trip coming up. We had him coming into the house in the evening, and he would tell us the names of everything in the room: windows, stoves, chairs, things like that. And we would write them down phonetically and practise them at night, and then go and try them on the Indians in the morning at schools. You know, it's a very dangerous thing to do because a little spirit of fun can turn language into something very different from what you think you're saying. However, they laughed with glee, and apparently we were directed right because the children did learn, and then we would tell them what it meant in our language. And their parents told me later that they would play school after school, and they would say all these words. And so, that was the way that we learned. We had to disregard all the methods that we had learned in Normal College and make— create our own way. So that is how we learned the language.

Now, I, staying at Aẏans, had in that village, 300 people. I had fifty-one pupils, and I was told before leaving Vancouver to take any age, any child that wanted to come in. Consequently, I had them from 3½ to 21. They were older than I was, but they were so eager to come that it would be a shame to turn them away.

The first day, Chief Derrick called a meeting of all of the village people in the council hall. And he told them that I was the representative of Mr. Government—they think it's one man. And that next to himself, in the village, I was to be chief. Great honour. And they were to obey me in everything I said. And if they didn't, he threatened them with terrific punishment. And that punishment was that they should be placed in the deep pit, the potato pit that's under each house—that's where they store their vegetables, down underneath the homes, you see—and filled in with straw. That was to be their punishment if they didn't do exactly as they were told. So, that's once I ranked next to an Indian chief.

The Indians were very kind to us. They brought us the first of everything they caught. The first rabbit of the season that was snared was brought to us. We had porcupine; that was brought to us, to eat. And we had the first of the catch of the oolichan fish. The oolichans, you know, are exceedingly rich smelts. They had them on the Skeena River, but the Nass is considered much richer, the fish is richer in oil. They brought us the first of that, they brought us the first of the salmon that they caught. And I didn't know at the time— we were thankful, we were grateful, because we had nothing but canned food ourselves that we'd taken up— but I didn't know until I read a book later, much later, that that was an honour accorded only to the chief. So there again, you see, we were honoured greatly.

Chief Derrick had been to Ottawa on a Royal Commission for something to do with lands or something like that. And he had travelled down the Great Lakes and was very much impressed by the saloon on those Great Lake boats, you know, long and narrow—the coloured windows. And he came home and he built himself a home, a very, very long hall in the front of this, a long room, and all around were red glass and blue glass and red glass and blue glass. This room became the school, the room that I taught in. Now at the back of this, on either side, were two little rooms. He lived with his old wife in one, and another family in that one. That child, by the way, was dying. But this was the school. In the centre of this room was a rather substantial stove, and they kept it warm with birch and ash and so on. I had plenty of wood; there was no lack of that. But the room was so large, that this stove right in the middle didn't give quite as much heat as we would've liked it to give.

And although the language was such a— the lack of knowing their language was such a barrier, we did make progress, however. And very soon they were actually reading from printing on the board, and

Ice fishing for oolichan on the Nass River. Photo: D-03105

understanding what they were reading, because if I would write instructions: "run to the steps" or "sit on the step" or such and such, they would do it, they understood and they could also write it and they could read it.

I had there fifty-one pupils on the roll, but not always. One day I went to school and I had three little tiny tots there. Nobody else turned up. So I went down through the village to inquire of the first person that could understand me, what had happened. And they said, this is a time when they go down oolichan fishing. And the whole tribe had packed up overnight and gone silently in their canoes down the river to fish oolichans from Fishery Bay; it's down towards the mouth of the river. And I didn't know how long they would be there, but I kept these three little tots as happy as I could for school, you know? And in due course of time, the villagers came back with all their empty cans—the coal-oil cans, they save those, they wash them out, they take the top off, put a handle of wood across and they go down to the fishing grounds with these. They catch the oolichans through the ice, they build fires on the shore and they render the fat from these fish, and then put it back into these cans, and come back loaded with this for the winter, or for the year rather; it's their lard for cooking, you use it in everything. And in due course of time, it becomes terribly rancid. And in due course of time, everything you have smells of oolichan fish. The wife of the chief used to put her big pan of bread to rise on the school stove, and over it would be a generous layer of oolichan grease. You couldn't escape it, wherever you went, was this horrible oolichan grease. They also brought back the fish and strung them on clotheslines; they're called candlefish, they're so heavy and fat that they had burned them in previous days as candles. So you'd see all these fish strung out on the clotheslines to dry stiff, and so on. That was one time when I hadn't fifty-one pupils.

The next time, I went, later on in the spring, and nobody was there again, so I had to find out. "Oh, this is the Moon of Strawberries; we plant strawberries." And so as I went out through the village over towards, to Gitlaxt'aamiks to go and see my friend—I might as well, there was no one at school—there I found them, away on the outskirts of the village, scratching the earth with hoes, not very deep cultivation, and setting out the little plants. I don't know where they got the plants in the first place, but evidently, somebody had got hold of some, and they were planting. And I thought Moon of Strawberries was Longfellow language, but they used it. And they didn't come back for two or three days, till they were ready to come back. And another time they were away, and this time I found that they were out gathering bark. It's something that they do every spring; they gather the bark from various trees, and some of it is medicinal, and the other, they used for weaving their baskets. And so, these are all community projects, you know. They do it all together.

I found in school now, the pupils were very attendant and most obedient. And they were very, very fond of music. And this missionary had evidently taught them a great deal of music. I think he was responsible for them having this band. And they would— my back was turned, and they were getting bored, they would suddenly burst into the most beautiful harmony. And they'd sing beautiful hymns, the old-fashioned hymns, you know, with a beat. [laughs] And the Indians were so interested in the fact that their children were getting education that they used to come stealing in through the front door. I didn't hear them half the time;

Some male members of the Nisga'a First Nation at Aýans, 1913. Photo: D-07858

they were all moccasined. And one old man, I remember, a grandfather, would come and silently walk up the whole length of the school to the front seat. We had forms, you know, just rows, no individual desks. And he would make his way up to this little girl's place, seat, and he would stand there looking down at her slate to see what she had accomplished. And he'd stand there quite some time, maybe ten minutes, and then he'd talk to her in a very quiet musical voice, and then his hand would go into his pocket and he'd bring out 50 cents and he'd put it down beside her on the desk. And away he'd go. That was her little reward. I think I should've been the one that got the reward, but he thought differently and she got it. And after school, how many friends she had. They all took her down to the little corner store, and they were with her until she bought this candy. I will say this about the children: if you gave one child a piece of candy, it would chop it into the tiniest pieces so that everyone could share.

Often, you know, when our well ran dry, we had to get water hauled from the river, and two or three of the boys would come with a sleigh, and they would take one of our tubs and haul it down to the river, and chop a hole in the ice, fill it and bring back to us. And as a reward— we usually made, we made a lot of candy up there—we'd make a big pan of fudge, or taffy, or something. And if they had colds, we would put a little eucalyptus oil into the taffy. They thought it was delicious. And they would always take it back and share it with every child in the village. Remarkable thing, you know. If you could see that done today, I don't know.

(5)

Life and Death in the Country

T HE NARRATIVE of British Columbia's settlement period is filled
with images of people arriving on boats, venturing out into the wilderness, and fulfilling their dreams of striking it rich or staking land.
The reality is that many people were ill-prepared for the conditions. With
so many diverse ecosystems—from deserts to tundra, prairies to canyons, mountains to coast—harsh winters and vast open spaces could be
quite unforgiving. Life or death could often be decided by one wise or
one poor decision.

From 1857 to 1914, just under 9,000 deaths were registered in British Columbia. Obviously, not every death was recorded, nor was the
smallpox epidemic that decimated most First Nations communities
represented in this number. In this same time period, only 7,320 births
were registered. With few doctors, especially outside of the major towns,
and only a budding infrastructure in place, the key to survival in British
Columbia was community. These stories highlight the role that friends,
family and colleagues played in everyday survival—even after death.

FACING: *A cattle ranch near Pavilion. The ill-fated cattle
drive from Carson Ranch in Pavilion took three months to
reach Vancouver, a distance of approximately 300 km.
Photo: 1-22335/BC Government*

It Was a Wild Ride

FLORENCE TRUDEAU

on the Birth of Her Niece

(RECORDED JULY 20, 1968)

FLORENCE "BUNCH" Trudeau (1918–2006) grew up in the remote Chilcotin community of Tatla Lake. Earlier in this book, she shared an anecdote about life as a child on the Chilcotin plateau and the tight bonds she had with her siblings and parents. Later in life, she and her sisters, Caroline and Jane, and her brother Alfred were still quite close and chose to live within several miles of each other. In fact, at the time of this story Bunch was living with Alfred on a ranch near 5 Mile (their parents' ranch), just outside of Anahim Lake. In this wide-open country where miles lay between houses, family members, including their father, Cyrus Lord Bryant, were their closest neighbours.

This story is about the birth of Trudeau's niece Marian Phyllis Waite (now Hargrove) on April 12, 1944. Ronald George Waite (1912–1979) was born in London, England, but left at age 17 with aspirations to be a rancher in Canada. Despite having no knowledge or experience of ranching, Waite worked his way across Canada on several ranches and farms and eventually became the head horsebreaker at the Gang Ranch in the Chilcotin. He married Trudeau's sister Caroline Josephine Bryant (1914–1969) (later Waite and then Moffat), and the couple had two children: Miles, who died a few days after birth, and Gloria, who drowned at the age of 2. Marian was their third child.

. . .

FACING: *A team of horses on the bank of the Chilcotin River, 1904. Photo: I-57594/Frank Cyril Swannell*

FLORENCE TRUDEAU: Marian was due, and we had a lot of fun with that. You see, we lived in a kind of a triangle affair. Alfred's place, where I was, was a mile and a half from Jane's. And on the other side was a mile and a half from Caroline's. But it was just in kind of a triangle affair. But you couldn't go from Jane's to Caroline's straight through because of swamp. You had to come over to Alfred's place, and then on through to Caroline's. So Caroline was expecting the baby. And it seemed to drop forward and be ready to come. So we were kind of expectant.

One night, Daddy and Alfred had gone to sleep, and I couldn't go to sleep. Something seemed to be haywire. So I was laying there. Suddenly I heard somebody call. A dog barked and I jumped up and ran, listened and I heard Ronald. And I answered him. So I went out and threw the saddle on my horse, and I took off. And it was in the 12th of, the 12th of March. And I took off at a high run, you see. And I got about half-way, and the road had thawed, leaving kind of a sideling bank of snow on the tracks. And my horse stuck his foot in a hole or something. And he

Bunch Trudeau's sister Caroline Waite (née Bryant) with baby Marian. Photo property of Marian Hargrove

turned end over end. And I got up. I was all right, just a little skinned. And he just lay there kind of moving his legs. And I thought, "Oh my gosh, a broken leg at this time." You know. He was an old horse. Then I saw him waggling all four legs and I knew he was all right. And I got him to his feet. But do you think he'd travel any faster than a slow trot? Not on your life. Anyway, I got over there, and I told Jane. And Jane went scooting her down through and she got pretty near to Caroline's and her horse stuck both feet in the spring hole, and he turned a cartwheel and she skinned all her face up. So I stayed and looked after the twins. And then I came over next morning and bathed the twins and got them all squared off, and Jane arrived. I said, "What is it, Jane? A boy or a girl?" "Just dress rehearsal." "Oh."

So we all met at the— or Caroline and Jane both came over the next Sunday. And we said

Ranch land at Anahim Lake, 1927. Photo: F-07963/*Frank Cyril Swannell*

we were going to have to get things straightened out so it was a little bit faster. So there was a fence or— between Caroline and our place, about halfway, and a gate you had to come through. So Ronald was to start over as soon as Caroline started having the pains. And he was to— as soon as he got to that gate, he was to start hollering. The dog would bark, and our dog would bark, and we'd jump up and we could hear Ronald. We'd answer him and he could go back— directly back to Caroline. And one of us would ride over to Jane's and when we got to the meadow, then that was about halfway. One would holler. We'd be hollering, and Jane's dog would hear and Jane could be on her way before we even got there, and leave all gates open. Everything was fine. So we waited. And we waited. And we waited. And I thought that kid was never going to come. One solid month.

And the night of the 12th of April, that night I couldn't go to sleep. Daddy and Alfred were sound asleep. And I heard the dog woof. I jumped up and I ran to the door and I listened and I heard Ronald holler. So I

Like her Aunt Bunch, Marian would grow to be very comfortable with horses. Photo property of Marian Hargrove

answered, good and loud so he knew it. Daddy was going to make the ride this time. Alfred said, "Do you want me to saddle your horse, Pa?" And he said, "No, I'll saddle him. I know where everything is and I'm all— and he's easy to catch." So he went down there and he grabbed— he caught Steele and he saddled him up. And we timed it, Alfred and I. From the time that Daddy left to saddle his horse—now it was a mile and a half to Jane's— and fifteen minutes from the time Daddy left to saddle his horse, Jane passed through. The dog barked at her passing through. And when she came back, it was a baby girl. Everything was all right. But boy, that was a wild ride, though, I'll tell you. And that's speed. We sure had it down to a fine art that time. [laughs] Oh, it was— so Marian always meant a little bit extra special to me after that.

We Can Starve Another Day

CHIEF FRANCIS EDWARDS

on a Cattle Drive to the Coast

(RECORDED OCTOBER 29, 1965)

CHIEF FRANCIS Edwards (1893–1973) was the son of a man with a Native name, who was called Edward in English. This is how the family name became Edwards. The older Edwards was born in Sechelt, but came to be living near what is now New Westminster. When the Hudson's Bay Company started to move furs and other goods toward Barkerville during the gold rush of the 1860s, many First Nations people were hired to work on the pack trains to move these goods through treacherous terrain. After many trips back and forth along the old Cariboo Road, the older Chief Edwards decided to settle near Pavilion after marrying a local woman. Pavilion got its name during the Fraser Canyon gold rush when the chief of the Ts'kw'aylaxw flew a large white cloth to signal to travellers that this was a friendly community.

Chief Francis Edwards grew up in a log house where his father kept a team of horses. When the salmon run began each year along the Fraser River, his father would hike down to the water and come home on each trip with sixty or seventy salmon. He and his wife would clean the salmon and then trade them with Robert "Old Man" Carson, owner of the Carson Ranch, for bacon, beef, flour and sugar. In those days, they were free to hunt and fish as their ancestors had for generations. Furthermore, deer, salmon and game were bountiful, the government did not impose regulations and the family never did without.

Edwards was 13 years old when he started to work for Old Man Carson, stacking hay and helping with the horses for 50¢ a day.

Farmland near Pavilion, 1946. Photo: 1-22326/BC Government (1946)

This was a lot of money: at the time, Edwards claims that a pair of shoes cost $1.25 and a pair of overalls was 75¢. Old Man Carson wanted to ranch, so he asked the chief's permission to use a ditch built by miners prospecting on their way to Barkerville that carried water in from Pavilion Creek. The chief agreed with no strings attached. In return, Carson would butcher a cow every Christmas and give it to the chief to divide among his people. Even after Carson died many years later, his son George Carson and his grandsons continued that tradition until the ranch was sold in 1942.

Today, Pavilion is still a ranching community and its ranches are among the oldest land grants in the province. In the following anecdote, Edwards describes an ill-fated cattle drive from Pavilion to Vancouver, a distance of about 300 kilometres. Today, it takes five hours to drive, but this cattle drive took three months.

.   .   .

CD3, TRACK 2

CHIEF FRANCIS EDWARDS: I'm going to try to tell you all about this old fellow's driving from here to Vancouver; from the Pavilion mountain, Old Man Carson's ranch. They started from here, and early— right after July, I think. It's in the month of August when they left here, drove about 300 heads of beef, and they went through Shalalth, and they went through Anderson Lake, and they went through Mount Currie, going through Pemberton. From Pemberton, up from there, starting to go up the hill, rocky places. That's where they're having a tough time. They really have a tough time, and their man that's packing grub for them comes back and forward to Lillooet to get the grub, then go back and feed these cowboys. But sometimes he gets behind. He doesn't reach quite early enough for these cowboys, and they usually go starve.

In some places on the way, why, the cattles can't find nothing—can't find nothing—no grass, nothing but rocks. But anyhow, when they have to camp, they have to camp. Sometimes they get to a place where they

A cattle drive in the Fraser Valley in the 1890s. Photo: E-08487

can feed the cattles, maybe one, two days. They kept going. But one place after that, they really got stuck. There's three, four of them beef cattles that's got so tender on a bad trail, you know. And they grabbed them there, roped them down, and they got ahold of big gunny sacks, you know, and wrapped it on the poor steer's feet, and got up way and could walk then. He can walk a ways. Pretty soon they wore out the sack, and his hooves had come out through the sack again.

And one place they were there, where the cook stopped, he says, "I can't cook nothing no more. No more tea, no coffee or anything." Well, they kept going that day until they find a place where they can have a rest, and wait for this man that's packing the grub to them. And again, the next day he didn't show up. The next day after that, he didn't show up. And that's two days going they haven't eaten nothing. So the boss says, "If he don't show up again tomorrow morning, we're going to tie up one of these beef cattles, and we're going to skin one of his hind legs, and we're going to cut a bunch of steak out of that." "Oh," one guys says— one of the cowboys says, "No, I wouldn't do that. I wouldn't eat out of his meat unless he's dead. We'll have to skin him before I'll eat out of him. Not when he's alive. We can starve another day. We can wait another day." "Okay."

Well, the next day after that, pretty late in the afternoon, well, that guy came up, where they had some grub. They had some grub. That, between Pemberton and Vancouver, that's pretty close around down Squamish, you know, but right up on top of the mountain. All on top of the mountain, where they're going through there's nothing but trails, you know. And had they kept on a-going, they kept on a-going. Mind you, you know how many days it takes them from Carson Ranch to North Vancouver? Three month— three month took them before they land down there. And what they call beef, they're nothing but little bit of meat left on each one of them— beef cattle, you know? But I guess those— the cowboys wouldn't kill, wouldn't skin one of their beefs like to get something to eat out of it, unless they kill them.

Yes, they got down Vancouver. Well, I was a kid then when I heard about that story, you know, and I must have went away, and I didn't heard anything of how they come back.

And the Band Played

CONSTANCE COX

on Fulfilling a Friend's Dying Wishes

(RECORDED IN 1959)

MRS. RUXTON E. Cox (1881–1960) better known as Constance, taught with the Gitxsan First Nation in northern British Columbia and also served as an interpreter for several prominent anthropologists, including Marius Barbeau in the 1920s and Wilson Duff in 1958.

Born in Hazelton, Cox was was the child of Thomas and Margaret Hankin. Her father, a former Hudson's Bay employee, had founded the town and also provided founding investments in the cannery towns of Port Essington and Inverness. Her mother was of Tlingit ancestry and spoke seven distinct First Nations languages. To mark Constance's birth, her father sponsored a large $3,000 potlatch to present her to the Gitxsan population of Hazelton. And throughout her life, she learned many distinct languages and customs from her mother. Eventually, Constance married telegraphist R. Eddie Cox and moved with him to North Vancouver. It was while living there that she met Imbert Orchard, who was working as a script editor for the CBC. After seeing a program he'd made about the Klondike gold rush, she walked into his office and said, "I want you to know that I was there. You got the story all wrong." Orchard promptly proceeded to record Cox's story; it was the very first of the 998 interviews he would conduct over the next seven years.

As such, these recordings with Cox are among the only ones in the collection not recorded with Ian Stephen. They were recorded with Orchard's secretary's tape recorder. Remarkably, the interview still sounds quite good. It marks the genesis of Orchard's amazing collection.

In this anecdote, Cox discusses the frontier town of Barkerville, which in the 1860s was the site of British Columbia's second gold rush. With a population of more than 10,000 people, it was the largest settlement north of San Francisco at the time. She vividly captures the sense of isolation in these remote places and the value of a tight-knit community and camaraderie.

. . .

CD3, TRACK 3 CONSTANCE COX: After my father had come out from England, and my uncle, another uncle came out— Uncle Charlie Hankin. He came out to join the gold rush to Barkerville, and he became partner to Billy Barker, whom Barkerville was named after. And they worked in the mine, and in Barkerville, of course, like all mining towns, it had all the trimmings of a mining town. There was the dance hall, and there were the

Barkerville was at one time the largest settlement north of San Francisco.
Photo: B-06885/H. W. Warden

saloons, and all the trimmings that belonged to a wild mining town.

The lady that run the dance hall, her name was Josephine. I never heard her other name, but she was always referred to as Josephine. Well, it seemed like my uncle was a great friend of Josephine's, and Josephine didn't like it in Barkerville. She didn't like the cold winters. The cold winters bothered her. She always had a cold. So she took very sick one winter, and they found out she had lung trouble and there was nothing to do for her. They couldn't take her out— no transportation in the winter. So she just laid in bed until she died. And before she died, she sent for my uncle. And she made him promise very faithfully that when she died she wouldn't be buried in Barkerville, because she hated the cold winters. That her body would be sent to San Francisco. That was quite a request to make, because navigation and travelling was one of the most difficult things in those days—no roads and no proper boats or anything. But however, he faithfully promised her that she would be buried in San Francisco.

Well, in due course, Josephine died. And, of course, they couldn't take her out in the winter, so she was buried in a snow mound, and they covered her all up with snow, and they hired two men to watch the grave so that wolves or dogs wouldn't dig her out and eat her up.

So this went on the whole— She died in February, and they couldn't leave Barkerville until about June when the snow was left enough so they could travel. So in the meantime, he had written away and asked the authorities of how, and give him permission to take the body to San Francisco. So they wrote and said that she could not be shipped unless she was in a tin casket. So, of course, there was no tin in Barkerville, and no tinsmith. So they had to write to Yale. There was a tinsmith at Yale, and so they sent for the tinsmith. And he had two donkeys, which he loaded with tin, and he arrived in Barkerville. After a month and a half travel, he arrived. Of course, he was getting paid by the day, so I don't suppose it bothered him just how long he travelled. So he got to Barkerville. He made the tin coffin.

And all the little bits of tin that was left over— he went to the beer parlour, or the saloon, and asked them, did they need beer jugs? That he had quite a bit of tin left over after making Josephine's coffin and he would make beer jugs. So the beer jug that I was fortunate enough to get from out of the saloon, it was patched in three places. Now you see how

Before a tinsmith settled in Barkerville in 1869, getting a tin coffin made was an ambitious enterprise. A-03774/Louis A. Blanc

carefully he used up every inch of the tin. So he made two dozen tin jugs, beer jugs, they were. And he sold them that, and then he made the tin coffin for Josephine, and Josephine was shipped to San Francisco.

She was brought from Barkerville. First of all, he hired two men to guard the spot where she was buried in the snow. Then he had to hire four men, eight men— four on and four off, to carry her into Barkerville. The tin coffin was lashed to a pole, and they carried the pole on their shoulders and they carried, walked from Barkerville into Yale. And that, I would say, was over 200 miles. And then she was put on the little boat at Yale and brought down to Victoria. Then he had to hire a man to accompany the coffin to San Francisco. In those days—I don't know if they still do it—but a coffin was never allowed to travel by itself. Somebody was to be strictly responsible. So he had to hire a man in Victoria to go to San Francisco with the coffin. So he hired this man, and Josephine eventually landed at San Francisco. And she had requested that a band attend her funeral. So a band had to be hired, and it cost $30,000 by the time he got her laid away in San Francisco.

I Will Die If You Keep Me Here

CONSTANCE COX

on Saving a Life at a Great Sacrifice

(RECORDED IN 1959)

THIS IS a story of both life and death that captures the vastness of British Columbia's wilderness. "Indian Isaac" was a full five-day trip by dog team from the closest settlement of Fort Babine when his 12-year-old daughter fell gravely ill. Her best chance of survival lay in getting her back to the fort and to the closest medicine, but the travel time meant infection or illness could go unchecked and lead to death. A surveyor in the area also fell ill around this time and pleaded with Isaac to take him to Fort Babine. Isaac only had enough space on his toboggan to transport one of them and therefore had to make a choice to save either his daughter or the surveyor. Isaac was rewarded with a medal for his efforts, but not without a steep cost. Central to this story are the care and camaraderie people shared, as a culture of helping one another was essential for survival.

Little is known about the Babine man known only to the government agents as "Indian Isaac." In July 1915, he had a case examined by the Royal Commission of Indian Affairs in which he stated that a "white man," telegraph lineman Billy Clark, had claimed his family land four years earlier. In his deposition, Isaac revealed that he lived in a house with a stable on a property at the north end of Bulkley Lake with his wife, three children and a nephew. His people, including his father and grandfather, had lived there for as long as he could remember. They had cleared and cultivated twenty acres out of a 250-acre property and kept fifteen horses and two cows. The railway ran between his land and the lake. While Isaac was out hunting, Clark had burned down Isaac's house and stable and all of his possessions. His wife's feet were badly burned while saving the children, and therefore Isaac sought out the Indian Agent for help and justice. Unfortunately, there are no records of what happened next.

Today, the Lake Babine Nation (also known as Nat'oot'en) inhabit a traditional territory around Babine River and Babine Lake in the Central Interior of British Columbia. The Babine River is a tributary of the Skeena River and is one of the top steelhead rivers in the world.

·   ·   ·

CD3, TRACK 4 CONSTANCE COX: I would like to tell you of quite a nice, interesting story about an Indian. And in fact at that time, he was the only Indian that ever had received a medal of any description. Now, this Indian received two: one from the Humane Society for saving a life of a surveyor, and the other was because he was the best Catholic in the village.

The story goes that Isaac—the French way of pronouncing, they always called him *A'zak*. So Isaac and his wife were heading for the hunting grounds. The hunting grounds was five days out of Babine. They lived at Babine. He had his wife and his two children and himself, and they headed for the hunting grounds. Well, they had arrived at the hunting grounds when the little girl, who was 12 years old, took very sick. She had pneumonia, and so they decided they'd return to Babine and take the girl back to Babine where she could get some medicine.

They had been camped there for a week, and they heard someone in the woods calling for help. And they didn't pay much attention to it at first, and his wife said, "That sounds like somebody in distress. They must be in trouble. Go, Isaac, and see." And Isaac said, "Well, maybe he's a long way from here." She said, "Well, it doesn't matter. You travel until you get there." So, he went, and he didn't travel any more than a mile. He met a man packing another man on his back, and it was a surveyor. He had pneumonia. So Isaac took him on his back and packed him and arrived in camp with him, and they put him in bed by the fire and gave him hot tea to drink.

And the surveyor said, "You must take me into Babine. I will die if you keep me here. I must be taken there. I must get medicine." So Isaac said, "Well, we're just going to take our little girl into Babine. I have only one toboggan and one lot of dogs." So, "Oh," the surveyor says, "but you must take me. I will pay you well. You must take me. Leave the little girl here, and then you can come back for her." So Isaac agreed, and put the man on the toboggan.

Now he, ordinary travelling, he was five days from Babine. But Isaac travelled night and day so that he was only three days getting back to Babine, and he lashed the dogs and they ran all the way. And he delivered the man at the Hudson Bay. And of course, the man got the medicine he wanted, and in no time he was better. Isaac, in a half an hour after he got there, they gave— The Hudson Bay gave him more food and fresh dogs, and he went back for the little girl. And when he got nearer the

The village of Fort Babine in 1923. Photo: F-07900/*Frank Cyril Swannell*

camp, he heard his wife crying and he knew then that his little girl had died, you see. So he got to the camp and he brought the body in. The surveyor, he was quite a, you know, a man with good character, and he gave Isaac $100 towards the little girl's funeral, and after he had paid him for bringing him in. And then, they buried the little girl, and the surveyor got quite well. So he returned back to Vancouver, and he reported it to the Humane Society that Isaac, at a great sacrifice, had saved his life—sacrificing the life of his little girl, you see.

So, in due course, a medal from the Humane Society was sent to Isaac. And at the same time, the Catholic Church had been looking over all the missions, and they decided that there should be a prize given to the best Catholic. So Isaac fell in line. The Catholic Church sent him a medal, you see, for being the best Catholic.

Isaac, of course, was very proud of these medals, and took them—The Hudson Bay, they were sent to the Hudson Bay manager, and in the presence of all the village they were to be pinned on Isaac: one from the Humane Society and one from the Catholic Church in Rome. So, Isaac was a little bit leery about the medals. He didn't understand them and he just didn't see why he, of all people—he was very humble in his village—and why he should get the medals. So, he went down to the Hudson Bay manager, and he said, "Are these medals really good?" "Oh, yes," the manager says, "they're wonderful, I wish I had them. If I only had one of them, I'd be satisfied. You keep them, Isaac, and you take good care of them. Some day if you get into trouble, those medals will help you out." Isaac thought, well, that was kind of wonderful. So, he brought them back, and he had them there.

And the Indians wouldn't talk to Isaac. If they met him on the street, they detoured around him. They didn't talk to him. So, his wife said, "That's those medals, you see? They're all going to hate us, and we'll die..." The Indians always think that if they're hated, they will die. So, she said, "Give them back." And he said, "No, the Hudson Bay manager said they were good, and that I was to keep them." Well, she said, "Look, nobody talking to us." So Isaac said, "Oh, I'll fix it. I'll give a feast at New Year."

So Isaac's idea of a feast was two barrels of homebrew. So he made this homebrew. When all the guests were there, and he said, "Now,

Isaac earned two medals for carrying a sick surveyor to the Hudson's Bay post at Fort Babine. Photo: D-06446/*Frank Cyril Swannell*

every time there's a round of drinks you must shake hands with everybody. This one shake hands with this one." So, they were shaking hands. But there was one man, he kept shaking hands with the same woman all the time. And, eventually the husband got jealous and stabbed this man in the back. So, the Mounted Police was called, and poor old Isaac was brought into Hazelton to stand trial for causing— making the barrel of homebrew, which caused the stabbing, you see? You always get arrested if you've caused it. You don't necessarily have to do the deed, but Isaac caused the stabbing, you see, by making the barrels of homebrew.

So, he was in jail. And, of course, soon as he arrived he asked the police if the police would go and get me. He said he was very down-hearted and he'd have to talk to me. So I was asked to go down, and I went. And I said, "Well, Isaac, what have you done?" "Oh," he said, "I didn't intend to do anything bad. I had a party, which I called the friend-ship party. I was going to bring back all my friends to me, and everybody was to shake hands." But he said, "Of course, this man made a mistake and kept shaking hands with the same woman all the time, and caused the trouble." He said, "If I get sent away to the white man's jail, I will die. I don't know anything about it," he said, "and I will die." And I said, "Oh, no, Isaac. They'll see that you won't die." I said, "It was very wrong of you

To restore his reputation, Isaac threw a New Year's Eve "feast" consisting of two barrels of homebrew, with unfortunate consequences. Photo: B-02778

to make homebrew. That's bad stuff. That makes people crazy." "Yes," he said, "I see now."

And I said, "Where are those medals you got?" "Oh," he said. "I've got them here. I've brought them along because— Just in case." So I said, "You give them to me." So Isaac gave them to me, and the ribbons were all torn and ragged and they were tarnished and dirty. So I took them home and I polished them. I polished them; they shone like diamonds. And my brother was in the war—he was in both world wars, and he had three medals given to him. So I took the ribbons off his medals. He didn't care for them anyway. Took the medals [sic] off, and put them on Isaac's. So I fixed them and I polished them and I took them down to the jail. And I said, "Now, Isaac, before you go into the courtroom..."—he was dressed very ragged—and I said, "Now, you pin this right here, and you stand up very straight and stick your chest out." And I said, "After that, we'll leave it to the medals."

So, court was called, and I was down there to interpret. The judge said to me, "Tell the prisoner to stand up." So I said, "Isaac, you're to stand up." And I said, "Don't forget about the chest: stick it out." So, Isaac stood very straight with the chest out, and of course— This judge, it was his first year on the bench. And he looked at the medals, and he said, "What

Isaac received a medal like this one from the Royal Humane Society for bravery. Photo courtesy of the Royal Humane Society

are those medals on his chest?" And I said, "Well, it's a long story but if you'd like to hear it, I'd be very glad to tell it to you." So, I told him the story of how Isaac got the medals, and he said, "Well, one for being the best Catholic and other for saving a life at a great sacrifice. Wonderful," he said, "wonderful." He said to the policeman, he said, "What did this man do that's why you arrested him?" Oh, by the time I got through telling the story, everybody was blowing their noses, you know, and feeling very sorry for Isaac. And so the policeman said, "Well, he made a barrel of homebrew." And so the judge said, "Well, is that the worst of crimes?" He said, "I made one myself one time, and wouldn't work, though," he said.

"No," he said. "Now, Isaac," he said, "I'm going to send you home to Babine." But he said, "Don't make any more homebrew. The policemen don't like it, I guess. Don't make any more," he said. "But I'm going to send you home." And he turned to me and he said, "Will you accompany us? We're going to have lunch with Isaac." He said, "I'm dining with Isaac today." Said, "I admire the man." So we went to the Chinese restaurant, and I had to go along to interpret the conversation during the meal. And he got Isaac a whole outfit of clothes and lots of groceries and sent him back to Babine.

I saw Isaac about twenty-five years afterwards. He was quite an old man. But the medals were still shining on the bosom when I met him.

I Found a Man Frozen to Death

BOB GAMMAN

on Transporting a Body for Burial

(RECORDED NOVEMBER 15, 1964)

ROBERT EDGAR Gamman (1882–1966) came to Canada in 1908 as a remittance man. Around the turn of the century, British custom dictated that first-born sons were entitled to the family inheritance. Many of the second- or third-born sons from wealthy families served as soldiers during the Second Boer War (1899–1902); however, when the war ended many became aimless. Jobs were scarce at the time, and so many of these sons were given a remittance, an allowance, to live away from England where they could not disgrace the family. Many of them ended up in British Columbia, particularly in the Okanagan Valley.

Bob was born in Suffolk, England, and had run away from home at the age of 15 to join the army and fight in the war. He served as an artilleryman and was stationed in Malta, Aden (Yemen) and Gibraltar. Like other remittance men, he felt aimless after the war. He never aspired to make any money; rather, his priority was simply to live away from civilization in the outdoors. A move to British Columbia suited him fine.

Upon his arrival, Bob paints himself as having no plans. He was, as he would call himself, "a rolling stone," and he was quick to find adventure. However, he is also quick to point out that no one could survive in British Columbia on their own. Newcomers had to learn from those with some experience living in such unforgiving environments.

.   .   .

BOB GAMMAN: I was in the country in 1908, the winter of 1908, in February. I came up from the States. I left the old country to stay with an uncle of mine in Chicago, my father's brother, and I didn't like that life, city life. So I gradually worked my way over to this coast. I wanted to be a farmer, of course, and I had a year on a farm, and I was as green as grass. [laughs] But my boss was a real gentleman. He never got mad with me. I had runaways, and goodness knows what, smashed the thing. But he never touched a thing when I was in a jam; he'd tell me what to do. He never touched a thing, and I learned an awful lot, I really did. I got so I was really efficient. In a very short time, I was driving four-horse teams and what have you. They don't— These farmers don't bother whether you're green or not, they say, "Here, take the team and go."

I was intending to go to Summerland. My father knew a farmer who used to be our neighbours at home, who came out here a long time ago, and that was an introduction, of course. Well, I went to see him, the damn man, [laughs] and he wasn't particularly friendly, and so I says, "To heck, I'll go somewhere else." So I hooked up and went to Vernon. And there I ran into a bunch of men of my type, who were nondescripts and ne'er-do-well, were rolling stones, and so on. And I had a wonderful time. I trapped. And I prospected. And I broke horses, and I did everything under the sun. I would be about 26, and I had a wonderful time.

And talking about trapping, I didn't know the first thing about it, you know, I said, well, "Get yourself a half a dozen traps, and go up in that mountain up there." Well, off I went. And I was trapping on another man's line. I caught a mink that morning. I didn't know how to kill the darn thing. You don't shoot them because you spoil the hide putting a hole in it. So I was wise to that. I took a piece of baling wire along, and I snared it after a time. That thing fought like, oh, terrific thing. And who should come along, but the man who owned the trapline. Well, normally, he could've done— put me in jail, but I explained to him my position, that I was a greenhorn and I was interested in trapping, and he was quite decent about it, showed me what to do. But I never went back there again, I wasn't allowed to. Oh, no, you're not allowed to trap within a mile or two of another man's line.

Well, I'm naturally a woodsman. I'm naturally an isolationist, and it

The city of Vernon in Bob Gamman's time, 1909. Photo: B-03298

appealed to me 100%. I lived in a cabin by myself for the first winter I was here. And I was as green— I didn't know how to cook anything. I'd met a man who had been all over the world, a real character he was. And he said to me, "What are you going to do this winter, Gamman?" I said, "I don't know. I'd like to stay here somewhere." Well, he said, "You can have my cabin." "Where is it?" "It's on the west side of the lake, opposite Okanagan Centre. You're on the old pioneer trail that ran from Okanagan and canted up to Kamloops. You'll never see anybody. There's a cabin there, there's a boat there, there's wood and there's a rifle. Go in." And I did. And I nearly froze to death. It was twenty below zero up there that winter, and I had a cabin as big as this room, with a big cookstove in it. But you can't heat a cabin with a cookstove. Now, I slept on the cookstove to keep warm. [laughs]

Well, the very first morning I was there, I shot a deer outside the door, and I honest to God didn't know what to do with it. I'd never shot a deer

Passing the winter in an unheated cabin, Bob Gamman slept on the cookstove to keep warm.
Photo: F-05038/Maynard

before. I didn't know how to skin it; I didn't know anything about it at all. So I left it. My nearest neighbour was a little store four miles away, and I figured on going down that afternoon and asking about it, and just getting someone [laughs] to show me what to do. But that night a logger came along the trail about suppertime, and he asked me how he could get to Kelowna. Well, I said, "You're too late for the ferry, you'd better stay with me." So he stayed with me for a week. And before supper, I told him about the deer. He fixed it up for me, took the hide off and cut up the joints, and I had meat. And he made me snowshoes and he showed me lots of things that I didn't know anything about: how to fell a tree and all sorts of things. A very fine man, he was.

Well, that country was full of that sort of people: wealthy boys, remittance men—lots of them—but they'd all had experience. They'd hunted in Africa, they'd been to India. How they ever got back, why they ever came to Canada, I don't know. But they were real men, they really were. They were wonderful people. You don't see them now. Of course, I'm out of the run of the things now, but there may be a few around the country. But they were really people you could depend on. And money, and— that was nothing, that was the least of their troubles. [laughs]

IMBERT ORCHARD: Did anything else happen in that cabin?

GAMMAN: I met— yes, I found a frozen man, a man frozen to death. And this man, above all things, had been the cook on the Alaska Boundary Survey for three years, living in that godforsaken cold country, and he comes down to the Okanagan and freezes to death. And I found him.

ORCHARD: What was he doing?

GAMMAN: Well, I'll tell you the story. There were several bachelors around about in cabins, and his name was Starkey. He was an Englishman. And he had farmed in Kansas, and his cousin ran the little store where I was telling you about close by. He was staying with him. Well, he promised to— he's a cook, you see, naturally he's a cook, and he promised to cook our Christmas dinner in one of the cabins—the biggest cabin there was in the country, up in the hills right about. And he was cooking, and one man, one of the gang, went to town to get the hooch. And the wrong man went. He was a quarrelsome fellow, he wasn't very popular, he came back tight. And annoyed Starkey very much, interfering with his cooking. So Starkey just packed up and went.

Well, that next morning—I didn't know all about this until I went up the next morning to see how they were getting on about Christmas Eve— and they said to me, "Have you seen Starkey?" I said, "No, where is he?" "He left here yesterday afternoon. We don't know where he is." "Oh." I said, "He's living with his cousin." "Well, we know where he was living." So I went back to his cousin's, to the store. I said, "Is Starkey home?" "No. Don't know where he is." Well, I'd been in the country long enough to notice conditions, and it snowed in the night. And I wasn't a 100 per cent perfect person, but I saw tracks that had been filled up with snow in the night, just by luck, going off the trail down the hill. And I followed those things, and there he was, frozen solid under a tree, with his pipe in his mouth, his hand behind his head and his legs crossed, frozen solid. And it was only four below zero that night. So I went back to the store, I said, "I found Starkey." So we got a sleigh, and dragged him down to the shop.

The next thing that was to do: bury him. Well, the nearest cemetery was Kelowna, and the only way to get him there was either by rowboat or tugboat or something. What were we going to put him in? No lumber. Well, this old chap at the store had a big old-country what we used to call wash basket, a basket about two-and-a-half to four feet, I suppose. Made of, you know, not wood but straw, or whatever you call it. Wicker, that's the word. And we could get his body in, not his legs. I'll tell you what I had to do: I had to break his legs, both his legs off at the hip, and tuck them behind his head like he was a chicken, and put the lid on. It was rather gruesome, but that was the only thing to do. Then how were we going to get him to Kelowna? Well, tugboats run the lake; they're hauling logs all the time. And we put him on a boat and I rode him out to a tug, and I told them to take this body to Kelowna and hand it over to the police. And we never heard anymore about it. Till about three years later. He was a Scotsman. His mother, who was about 90, came all the way from Scotland to Kelowna to see his grave, have a stone erected and go home again. Isn't that extraordinary?

That was pathetic, you know. I committed a crime, but what else could you do? No one ever knew what I did. Well, he just cracked like a stone, you know, he was frozen solid. But that's the only way we had to put him away. We had no lumber. We had a few nails, probably, but there was nothing in the country, then, nothing convenient.

(6)

A Suitable Place for a City

BRITISH COLUMBIA is not really a single place. There is as much variety in geography to be found within this province's borders as in the rest of Canada. Although the province was settled much later than Ontario or Quebec, its growth was more rapid. Most of the population was speckled across a number of small resource-based communities, port communities and arable farms. By 1911, only four cities had more than 4,000 residents: Vancouver (population 100,401), Victoria (31,660), New Westminster (13,199) and Nanaimo (8,306), leaving 230,000 people in smaller locales.

The stories here focus on the early days in those smaller communities. While much of the history of this province has focussed on the policy-makers in Victoria and a few exceptional characters, examining the history of these smaller areas illuminates the spirit of its people. What is common among these stories is how each town was shaped by its landscape and its visionary settlers. These recollections remind us just how unique and diverse are the people and places that make up the province.

FACING: *A CPR engine pulling into Vernon station.*
Photo: B-00224

They Came Scarce

AGNES RUSS

on the Shaping of the Masset Reserve

(RECORDED SEPTEMBER 10, 1962)

THE PRIMARY speaker in this interview is Grace Stevens (1884–1973), and she is translating for her mother, Agnes Russ (née Hubbs, 1857 or 1859–1964), who speaks mostly in a Haida dialect. Both women were from the Haida First Nation on the Queen Charlotte Islands (Haida Gwaii), and Agnes Russ lived most of her life in the town of Masset. For the sake of the recording, some of the Haida dialect has been edited to keep the flow of the narrative in English.

Before a Hudson's Bay post was established in Masset, Charles Hubbs, an American, ran the trading post there. He fell in love with the chief's daughter, whose name we don't know, and Agnes was their child. However, Charles Hubbs had aspirations of following the Cariboo gold rush of the early 1860s, and his father-in-law would not let Agnes's mother go with him unless they left the baby behind. Agnes's parents therefore left her to be raised by her grandparents, and she was accorded all the status and luxury of a chief's granddaughter, including owning several slaves. She was a survivor of the smallpox epidemic of 1862.

At a young age, Agnes Hubbs married a chief who died before the two started a family. She later entered the Crosby Girls' Home, which was operated by the Women's Missionary Society of the Methodist Church, in Fort Simpson, where she met her second husband, Gedanst. He was born in Skidegate, also on the Queen Charlotte Islands, but was later baptized Amos E. Russ, the namesake of a pioneer Methodist preacher. To escape

FACING: *Hunting sea otter, 1915.*
Photo: D-08364/Edward Sheriff Curtis

155

the fury of his grandfather for having accepted Christianity, Russ had fled to Fort Simpson. He later became the Native constable of Skidegate and was instrumental in the conversion of many Haida to Christianity.

In this interview, Russ discusses the formation of the Masset Indian Reserve on the northern coast of Graham Island, the largest island in the Queen Charlotte Islands archipelago. An Indian reserve is a parcel of land set aside by the Crown for the exclusive use of an Indian band. It is important to note that reserve lands are not owned by the bands but are held in trust by the government. In the late 1860s, just after many of British Columbia's reserves were formed, the Governor of British Columbia, Joseph Trutch, "cut off" what he deemed to be excess land from many reserves. He believed that the land could better serve non-Native settlers. Amos Russ lobbied for the Old Massett Reserve to expand in size due to the influx of Haida coming to the area.

· · ·

CD3, TRACK 6 GRACE STEVENS: Yes, of course her family, as I told you before, they were, they owned certain portions of land from point to point as it were, or from inlet to inlet. And her people's property was on the west coast

The village of Masset, in the Queen Charlotte Islands. Photo: D-04196

where nobody could hunt there by land or sea from that strip of property and that's where her young husband went to hunt sea otter. She remembers one summer they went there, they got six sea otter and they brought one young one home to her to play with. She says they were there. When they're young, they're white and she had that for a pet to play with for a long time.

She says that when the flood came, of course it wasn't in her time, but her grandmother's grandmother used to tell about it and hand it down to her by her grandmother. They were out living in this place I'm telling you about on the west coast. And the flood came, the land was covered for twenty days and they got into canoes and anchored to the highest peak behind the village. And they claim that they used to see the rocks that they had tied to on top of this hill anchored there for twenty days, she says.

Reverend Amos E. Russ, ca. 1880.
Photo: B-04728

She says one of her very ancestors from way back, a woman, came down. She had this, this cane, I guess, and she put this in the ground and she sang ten songs belonging to her ancestors and her family. And she stood and did this and sang these ten songs and then when she pulled the cane out of the ground, there was a spring that shot up of water, fresh water. And she says that spring is still there, she's seen it herself. It comes right out of the ground spurting up. She says if you went out there, you could see it, too.

She said that she could, it would take too long to tell you everything she's heard about the flood, regarding her own family and how they've gone: some went to Alaska and some went to the south end of the island. They still recognize the family ties. It isn't really family, but it's the, her own tribe that scattered. Some went to Alaska and some went to the south end of this island. And some stayed right in their own, in Masset.

When Judge O'Reilly and his party come to, to survey out the reserves on the Queen Charlotte Islands, yes, my father joined them. They got my father to come with them as an interpreter. There was Judge O'Reilly and there was a Chinaman cook and she says that there was five or six

Judge Peter O'Reilly, who led a survey group in the Queen Charlottes, ca. 1860. Photo: A-01104

surveyors, and so my father had to talk with the judge and asked him to make this reserve a little larger if he could, which he did. They gave him quite a welcome when he came here. Of course, they didn't understand all the ins and outs of everything. They gave him quite a welcome. They fired off cannons as to welcome him. The chiefs put on their best clothes and he was very pleased with that. So he told my dad that he would make this reserve larger. And they sold the timber off of this reserve, which helped them to lay it, improve their village, you know, the waterline and other things they have done. The chur—, the hall, the town hall was built from the revenue.

They came scarce, you know. The people died off and went away and there wasn't enough to keep up villages, I suppose, and they decided all to come here. Kloo people came here first. I remember that. And then Maude Island people came here, Gold Harbour village came here. Of course, they asked permission to come first, and they were invited by the chiefs. And she thinks that that's why their people here are better off than, because it's through, through, the Methodist Church coming here that they have the church and the hospital.

The Landing in the Bay

GRACE CHAMBERLIN

on the Early Days in Gibsons

(RECORDED JUNE 17, 1965)

MARY GRACE Chamberlin (née Glassford, 1890–1979) is the grand-daughter of George William Gibson, Sr. (1829–1913), the founder of Gibsons Landing on the Sunshine Coast. Gibsons, as it is now called, is the marine gateway to the Sunshine Coast. Although it is located just thirty-three kilometres from Vancouver, Gibsons is not accessible by road from the Lower Mainland. The community is best known as the setting of the CBC television series *The Beachcombers*.

George Gibson was born in Lincolnshire, England, but ran away to sea at the age of 12. He reached the rank of lieutenant in the Royal Navy before settling in Chatham, Ontario, where he married Augusta Charlotte Purdee and took up gardening while raising eight children. Wanting land of his own, Gibson headed west with two sons to stake a pre-emption. They landed in what is now Gibsons in a homemade boat named *The Swamp Angel* on May 24, 1886. After he had established a community, donated land for a school and cemetery, and worked as postmaster there, the settlement took on the name Gibsons Landing in 1907 in his honour.

Chamberlin was the third of seven children born to George Glassford (1856–1942) and Mary Ann Gibson (1865–1937), George Gibson's second daughter. The Glassfords moved to British Columbia in the mid-1880s from Ontario, but they did not care for Vancouver. In fact, Grace recalls that her father called Vancouver "the most awful-looking place he ever

159

saw; Vancouver was nothing but charcoal and wet." After three years, he took up a 160-acre pre-emption at Grantham's Landing, a short distance from Gibsons Landing. Every Saturday, Glassford commuted to Vancouver in a rowboat carrying cordwood cut from his property to sell in the city. This is how he made ends meet.

Along with his brother-in-law, Ralph Gibson, and his father-in-law, George Gibson, Glassford set up the first stores, Methodist church and schoolhouse in Gibsons Landing. By virtue of their camaraderie and sharing, these families were instrumental in successfully building the community.

.   .   .   .

George Glassford and his family, 1909, moved to Gibsons Landing because he thought Vancouver "was the most awful-looking place he ever saw." Photo: c-05352

GRACE CHAMBERLIN: I was born May the 12th in 1890 in Gibsons. CD3, TRACK 7
Well, at that time they called it Howe Sound. You see, Old Man Gibson
was my grandfather—his name was George William Gibson—and he
took up his property in 1885, but I don't think he came here to live until
about 1886. He was an old man when he came here, I think he was—
wasn't he 60 years old when he came here? Oh, he just loved it. And he
had always been a farmer in Ontario; before he came to Ontario he had
been a sea captain or a sailor on windjammers.

IMBERT ORCHARD: Why did he come west?

CHAMBERLIN: Didn't everybody come west because it was a wonderful place to come? In the '80s, well, everybody was going to get rich out
there. [laughs] Old Mr. Gibson and his two sons came by way of San
Francisco and came up from there to Vancouver. Well, then of course
they were there when the big fire was, in 1886. And then his wife and
family, and my dad and mother all came in 1886, in
October.

Oh yes, Old Mr. Gibson built himself a boat, I think
over in Oyster Bay on Vancouver Island. And he and his
two sons were coming to Vancouver and they got out in
a storm, a very bad storm, and so they got on the Gulf
of Georgia and they couldn't find their way very good. It
was so rough, and so they saw the gap coming in and they
came in the gap and he landed in the landing in the bay.
And thought it was so wonderful—it was something like
some old place in England that he knew—that he decided
he'd pre-empt here if it was possible. And then he pre-
empted and his sons pre-empted. Well, one took— Paisley
Island was one son's property; the other one took here.

ORCHARD: Was there any other white settlement in the
whole of Howe Sound in those days?

CHAMBERLIN: There weren't very much of any kind of
settlement. There had been people living here; there'd
been logging camps, because there were lots of old

George William Gibson, Sr., with his
wife Augusta Charlotte Gibson (née
Purdee) and their dog. Photo from the
Harbour Publishing archives

A skid road was one of the few ways to get around in the early days of Gibsons, 1904.
Photo: 1-33655/Frank Cyril Swannell

bones as I can remember, of old bull teams. I can remember when I was a kid, Old Mr. Dupree, he logged down a skid road here with bulls, you know, with those yokes on their necks, hauled logs down? They'd logged and gone, I presume.

When I first was a kid, there was only a trail going across. My grandfather lived at the head of the wharf, and we used to just run through the trail. The only road I remember was coming up the hill and that wasn't very good, you know, the school road like.

We moved away from the bay and then there was the Indian reserve down between us and Grandpa's. Mother said when I was a baby the Indians all came to see me. They thought that I guess I was some kind of a— something new! Oh, there were lots of people at one time, but they dwindled down to a few families again because there was no way to make a living. And a lot of people left the landing.

The first store was my uncle's, Ralph Gibson. That was the first store. That was in '93 or '94. Well, he had groceries and that's about all, just groceries and flour and feed and that kind of thing, for chickens and cows. My grandfather built a store right at the head of the wharf but about 1910, I think, it burned down.

Old Mr. Gibson, he was a big, tall, six-foot-four man with a very good personality in many ways, but I was always a little scared of him because I thought he was bossy. He was a very honest man, I think, but he also was a man that wanted things his way. But he was JP [justice of the peace] for many years, of the community, and he was a very conscientious old man, though. People used to come when the boats came in and there was no place for them to stay, well, it was, "Come into my house and help yourself," you know, eat and sleep until the boat got there. You know, if he killed an animal, well, he thought he should divvy it around. For many years, you know, the old-timers did that sort of thing, and if they had a loaf of bread and somebody else didn't, they'd pass it around.

At one time Dad said that there wasn't only a half a loaf of bread in the whole community because my grandfather had the only boat to go over to Vancouver in, the one he built, you know, and he went to Vancouver and it was so rough they couldn't get back, and nobody had any flour and nobody had anything. But eventually they got back and all had something

Gibsons Landing, 1930s. Photo: B-07552/Helen McCall

to eat then. But that was before I could remember. Things weren't bad like that when I was little.

Oh, my grandfather had a fairly good clearing. He had all kinds of fruit trees planted as long as I could remember; rhubarb, raspberries, all that kind of thing. He sold a lot of that sort of thing afterwards, to the boats, you know, that came in. First there was the *Comox*, the *Capilano*, those were all the Union boats, that's the first I remember coming. But before that people used to go up and down on tugboats; they'd come in and they'd take the tugboat in to Vancouver. And they'd go— come here, then go north. Well, you never knew when they were coming back. On their way back they'd call in and pick up the passengers and stop, but that's the way we got our mail going up, put it on coming back.

Oh, it wasn't a bad life. It was pretty good! And we always had all we wanted to eat.

A Beautiful and Natural Fertile Land

LEON LADNER

on the Founding of Ladner

(RECORDED FEBRUARY 1964)

IN THE following anecdote, Leon Johnson Ladner (1884–1978) describes how his father, Thomas Ellis Ladner (1836–1922), along with his father's brother, William Henry Ladner (1826–1907), founded the town of Ladner in 1868. The two men had been in British Columbia for ten years and had acquired 1,200 acres of farmland in the Fraser River Delta. They were the first Europeans to become permanent settlers in the area.

Ladner's Landing (later called Ladner) was created as a fishing and farming village on the banks of the Fraser River. A post office was opened there in 1875, and the Delta Canning Company was opened by Thomas Ladner in 1887. Today, Ladner and its suburban neighbour to the south, Tsawwassen, make up the unofficial region known as South Delta, a suburb of Vancouver.

Thomas and William Ladner both left Penzance, Cornwall, with their father in 1851 to follow the gold rush in the United States. Thomas was only 16 years old at the time. While travelling in Wisconsin, their father died, but the brothers continued west across the United States for five months and six days before they landed in the Sierra Nevada Mountains. Thomas got a job driving a democrat team, which is a covered wagon, and the brothers mined in California for six years until 1858, when they got wind of the gold rush up in British Columbia.

In this story, Leon Ladner mentions a dispute between his father and uncle and Governor James Douglas. Douglas was the Chief Factor of the

Hudson's Bay Company back in the 1850s and eventually became the second premier of British Columbia. A very powerful man, he set out to pass several laws to try to keep what would eventually become an enormous gold rush as organized as he possibly could. Approximately 30,000 miners came up to British Columbia in the summer of 1858, and Thomas and William Ladner were among them.

. . .

CD3, TRACK 8 LEON LADNER: My father, he didn't like Governor Douglas. Governor Douglas was a very good administrator but austere, haughty and a bit arrogant at the time. He knew him quite well; however, the brothers couldn't get across the Gulf. My father at that time would be about 18 and his brother, 29, William Ladner. They couldn't get across the Gulf of Georgia. So many people, at least 30,000 Americans in the gold fields in Victoria. So my dad and uncle being very resourceful, typical strong, virile English people, decided to go to an Indian chief near Victoria and have him build a big war canoe and take them over in the canoe, just as the Indians crossed and had done for hundreds of years to the fishing grounds around Point Robert [*sic*].

Sir James Douglas, chief factor of the Hudson's Bay Company and later premier, ca. 1860.
Photo: F-07680

They made a deal, half the money down when they left, half when they got to Tsawwassen, but before they started they found out that Governor Douglas had put on a levy, a duty and a tax, on all boats going into the Fraser River and had placed a gunboat there. This was aimed chiefly at the Americans who came up and contributed nothing to the revenue, but my father being an Englishman coming to a British Colony thought this was a bit highhanded. He objected to it. They charged $5 a head and then 10% on everything they brought in.

Governor Douglas was Chief Factor of the Hudson Bay. He had an authority over property, fur trading and things like that, but some of his authority was greatly limited as governor of the Hudson Bay. My father, in some way or another, knew about this and he knew perfectly well he had no right to put the gunboat in the mouth of the Fraser River because he had no jurisdiction as governor. He only had jurisdiction as the Chief Factor of the Hudson Bay. But as Chief Factor of the Hudson Bay, he had no right to put in gunboats and hold people up and take money from them. So that aroused a great deal of interest at that time. So he didn't like this. And then he said, well, he'll fix this. He will avoid the Fraser River.

So just off the mouth of Fraser River or Canoe Pass, I've forgotten which it was, he cut loose. In accordance with the agreement, Father and Uncle were landed at an Indian reserve that was part of the agree-

ment. Whereupon, the brothers had to pay the Indians the balance of the money. They got on the reserve. To their great surprise the Indian chief got in his canoe and went away because this was in the evening time. They found out instead of being landed near Fort Langley, and that was the place they were going to, they had been landed at Tsawwassen, thirty-five miles from Fort Langley. Well, that was a problem. So they had to walk and you can imagine them that night how they steamed over this but could do nothing because the Indian was far out in the water.

They got porters and they walked across Delta, and as they were walking across—either at Langley or at the Boundary Bay where they got out of the canoes, I've forgotten which—as they were walking across, they saw this beautiful and natural fertile land. And in May it wouldn't be much water on it. One brother said to the other, "When we've made our

Thomas Ellis Ladner, ca. 1860, founded the town of Ladner in 1868. Photo: G-07397

William Henry Ladner, ca. 1863, Thomas Ladner's brother and the co-founder of Ladner. Photo: A-01409/Hannah Hatherly Maynard

money in gold mining in the Cariboo, we'll come back here to settle and take up this land. We will tell nobody."

So they continued on to Fort Langley, went up to Fort Hope and then my uncle and father engaged— they tried mining for a while on the river but it was no good. So they then went into the transportation business. They got sixty, sixty-five mules and they carried freight, first from Yale to North Bend and then to Lillooet— I won't go into details. They charged at that time $1 a pound, and a mule would hold 250 pounds. And then after that they went into the Williams Lake and the Barkerville area, and until 1866 they did quite well. At first they only had a trail; there was no road. Then my uncle made a cutoff— put a lot of his money into it—and they made considerable money that way.

But one amusing incident took place. At Barkerville, a gentleman operated the store, quite an important store, and his name was David Oppenheimer and he became the mayor of Vancouver. He was the first mayor of Vancouver; you'll see his monument. And my father delivered freight to him. One day he went into the David Oppenheimer store and while there a man came in to buy a needle, and he said, "How much is a needle?" Oppenheimer said, "One dollar." "Good God," he says, "this is highway robbery. What are you doing?" The guy says, "Don't blame me. Look at that man, Tom Ladner, over there. It's the freight on the damn thing."

But the business went down, the mining went down, so about 1866 they came back to New Westminster and decided to carry out their intention of going to Ladner. August 8, 1868, it was at a place called the

Cohilukthan Slough, and this is the start of the delta and the start of Ladner and the start of what's there today. Uncle William had taken the land, as you will see by that design, west of the slough. In the end he had 640 acres. My father took 500 acres east of the slough, and that's where I lived nearly all my life.

Well, he took up this land and it was terrible. It was subject to floods all the time. The weather wasn't good. Some years they have twenty-six inches of rain in the year—the average is about thirty inches over there—but other years it would be fifty-eight inches. And they had very great difficulty with the land. They had to build their own dykes. They had to bring down their supplies, and my father being a Cornishman and a careful man with his money—he had money—he was conserving it and building it.

Later I will tell you about John Oliver who subsequently became premier of British Columbia and he is the one who solved the whole drainage system of Delta. About three feet under the ground he built a triangular-shaped drain made of cedar planks with the apex sticking up, and that took the water off in time in the spring so as to make it possible for the crops to be put in. But when my father started we didn't have that advantage. Well, being a businessman and a builder and a constructive thinker, he found that there was a cannery up near or beyond New Westminster that was doing quite well. And having some money he started in the cannery business, and that was his real and great occupation.

David Oppenheimer, a successful businessman in Barkerville who went on to become mayor of Vancouver, ca. 1880. Photo: A-02384/Imperial Studio

He started to build a cannery where the Cohilukthan Slough comes into the river, and he did extremely well there on that. Then they built another one at Canoe Pass, I won't give all the details, the Wellington Canning

By 1910, Ladner had grown considerably. Photo: E-00139

Company. Their business was highly successful. In the end they had eight canneries and they did very well. And I have here a photograph of the delta, what's called the Delta Cannery that's at Ladner and the scows and the Indian boats and wherever they could put it. There were between 75,000 and 100,000 salmon: they had to use salt to preserve them.

During this period the boats going between New Westminster and Victoria, there was no Vancouver, of course, used to stop at the farm and then at the cannery to let off freight. So they called it Ladner's Landing. Then they named was shortened to Ladner's and then it was later changed by the post office to Ladner.

No Place Like This

CORNELIUS KELLEHER

on the Beginnings of Mission City

(RECORDED MARCH 1963)

CORNELIUS KELLEHER (1872–1969) was the son of Irishman Mortimer Kelleher and a woman known only as Magdeleine, who was a member of the Nooksack First Nation of northwestern Washington State. Mortimer Kelleher felt compelled to leave Ireland because his father tried to force him to marry a "rich-monied" woman. After running away to sea, he landed in San Francisco in the early 1850s where he deserted the ship he was on to go to the gold fields. After the gold rush ended, he was enlisted in the American army to quell an "Indian uprising."

Kelleher Sr. moved north to British Columbia with word of the gold rushes of the early 1860s, first to Fort Langley. Never one to back down from a fight, in one incident Kelleher had the hat shot right off his head. After some time in the Cariboo, he made his way back south in 1868 and took up a ranch in Sumas Prairie. However, he could not manage the flooding waters on one side of the river, so he took up a ranch on the other side: the site of Mission City today. In order to make ends meet, Kelleher Sr. worked for the Oblates of Mary Immaculate (O.M.I) Mission, a common practice of ranchers in the area. In this way, the O.M.I. Mission got its grist and saw mills built and operating.

In 1861, Father Leon Fouquet was a representative of the O.M.I. on a quest to establish a residential school in the Fraser Valley. It was his charge to bring "the good news of Christianity to the Indian people." He founded the school and church called St. Mary's Mission in 1868.

Starting in 1879, Cornelius Kelleher was a student there. The thriving city of Mission grew up around this school.

Mission City is located on the north bank of the Fraser River, overlooking the city of Abbotsford, and is part of the central Fraser Valley. The name Mission City was chosen due to the site's proximity to the St. Mary's Mission of the Oblate order. That Mission is now the Peckquaylis Indian Reserve.

· · ·

CD3, TRACK 9 CORNELIUS KELLEHER: Father Fouquet said they came in '62, 1862, you see, when he landed at the creek there. I remember him very well, because I used to have lots of conversation with the old gentleman. And the last time I had them I was up at the mission, there, and we sat down there for hours I guess, talking about it. How he'd come up; they came over into Oregon, first—the O.M.I.—and from Oregon they drift over here to Vancouver Island. At Vancouver Island, he was delegated to come up the river, the Fraser River, to find a suitable place for to start a mission.

Well, he said, "I took twelve Indians down to New Westminster, and came up in a big Chinook canoe, and came to this place, here." He said, "When I come around the bend down there," he says, "I seen this little

Cornelius Kelleher with his wife, Julia Mathilda Kelleher (née Wells), in 1948. Photo: B-07898

hill, and nice place, and flat land across the river." He says, "That's the place I'm going to have." So he says, "We landed at the creek." The Mission Creek now, they call it. And he says, "We had cook our dinner— dry salmon, you know, and some potatoes we had." He says, "And I *cultus coolee* around the back." What he meant, in Chinook, was that he was going to take a look around. He told the Indian, "*Nika tikkee cultus coolee nanitch*," he says. "*Bymby mamook house*," you know he says.

IMBERT ORCHARD: What's that mean?

KELLEHER: Means he was going to build here, you see? [laughs] He got in after they had their lunch, and they had had a look around the woods, there, you know, and places where they thought there— He said, "We got in the canoe, and we went all up the river. Way up Fort Yale," he says. There were no Fort Yale then, only Indian places. He says, "And we come back." He says, "I see no place like this." So he says, "We started here." So he says, "We come back up, and I went back down to New Westminster and over to Victoria, to the headquarters that were there." Bishop D'Herbomez was the head bishop there then. Well, he says, "We made arrangements to come up and start."

He says, "And I got a bunch of Indians with me," he says. "And Brother Ryan, and old Brother Varnier. We come up and started log houses, you see, where we could live in, and Indians had log houses too." But he says, "We never paid the Indians anything." He said, "They lived on us, and they were glad to help us." He got the Indians to whipsaw the lumber, you see? And here were the logs for their houses, you see, for their log houses.

Father Leon Fouquet, 1859, founded the St. Mary's Mission school and church that eventually developed into the city of Mission. Photo: 1-51542

You see, when I first come there in '79, our schoolroom was a little log house, you see. And the rest of the places, you know, they were just cutting enough lumber to build what we used to call the priest's house, you know. They built a big house there where the clergymen had their own rooms, and their chapel, and so on. And our schoolroom wasn't built yet, then, you see. They had built a great big chimney in the one end of it, you know, with rock.

This Brother Varnier, he was quite a man. He could turn his hand to most anything, you see. He got the rock, and mixed up clay, and lime, and straw, and all kinds of things, and built a big chimney there. Great big place, fireplace in there, with an iron bar across it— I don't know where they got it. When I was talking about the great, big brass kettles— the way they used to cook the soup, and boil the beef and the potatoes, and the vegetables in it, you know. I don't know what happened to them. They hung over the fireplace, you know, this stone fireplace, where they cooked their stuff like that.

Mission City, ca. 1900. Photo: B-07886

A Wide Spot in the Road

JAMES INGLIS

on the Growth of Lumby and the Flying Frenchmen

(RECORDED MAY 16, 1965)

JAMES WILSON Inglis (1897–1976) was born in Lumby, now known as the gateway to the Monashee Mountains, which are located in the northeast corner of the Okanagan Valley. Before European contact, the Okanagan and Shuswap First Nations had gathered food and fished in the area for thousands of years. The first man to pre-empt land at Lumby was Peter Bessette, and other French Canadians followed. Men like Louis Morand eventually built stores and hotels as the townsite grew, making it a predominantly French Canadian settlement when it was first established. This was unique among British Columbia's frontier towns. The J.W. Inglis Elementary School in Lumby was named for James Wilson Inglis.

David Inglis, James's father, was born in Lanarkshire, Scotland, in 1854. He was a farmer and later a miner, and he moved to Illinois to work in a coal mine. There he married an Englishwoman named Elizabeth Wilson in 1886, and James was the fifth of six children born to the couple. Like many miners of the day, David Inglis contracted "rheumatism." (The term "inflammatory rheumatism" is no longer recognized by doctors today but is often used in historical context.) He suffered from aching joint pain, likely as a result of poor ventilation and hard conditions in the mines, and was badly affected by the damp weather. Apparently, British Columbia's climate is perfect for those seeking refuge from this pain, and David Inglis eventually moved north with his family. His is one of many stories in the Orchard collection that tell of people who came to British Columbia for health reasons.

175

This anecdote also discusses The Flying Frenchmen hockey club of Lumby. Two brothers from Nelson—Curtis Lester Patrick, known both as "Les" and the "Silver Fox," and Frank—created the Pacific Coast Hockey Association and helped develop several rules for the game, including introducing the red forward line that is still used on professional hockey rinks. Les Patrick played professionally with the Victoria Cougars and the New York Rangers, and his sisters played for the Nelson Ladies Hockey Club, which Les coached. The Lester Patrick Trophy is still awarded annually for outstanding contributions to hockey in the United States and until 1994, when the National Hockey League switched to Eastern and Western Conferences, it had a Patrick Division.

.   .   .

CD3, TRACK 10

JAMES INGLIS: I was born 1897. Yes, I was born right in the village of Lumby. At one time, the Board of Trade published that I was the first white child born in the village of Lumby. My dad, David Inglis, he came from Scotland just out of Dumfermline, came into Lumby here in February of '92 but they came with the Scottish miners to Illinois in the United States, a fluctuation of miners there for the industry—the coal industry that supplied the power, steam power—and they brought the Scottish miners in, and— I would say that probably '87. So it would be probably just before that, a couple years before that, when my dad came to the United States. He was married in the United States. My mother came from England.

He contacted [sic] inflammatory rheumatism through the mines and he became absolutely a cripple six months of the year in bed. And there was nothing they could do to help him, which we know is a terrible thing, and the doctor said the only hope he had was to move and keep on moving, and if it ever left him to stay there. Well, he moved across the United States into Washington and of course that didn't help. He was in the mines down here or in the little mining town of Puyallup, just out of Seattle, and someone, I don't know how this came about, but somewhere he met someone that told him about the Okanagan Valley and some old chap Baxter that lived up in the top end of Creighton Valley up at the 28 Mile post, and advised him he should go up.

In that year, in February, they put him on the train and he was walking with two canes, and he came up here. Got into Vernon, found out where this old chap was. There wasn't— there was a road in here but up in the top end of the valley there were practically none but a trail, and he headed off for Vernon— from Vernon to go up there and see this old chap Baxter. And he tossed his canes away and walked out there, and only once after that did he ever contact [*sic*] inflammatory rheumatism. And, of course, as the doctors say, if you ever find where it leaves you, stay there, and that is what brought him here. My mother followed him in here in June with— there was four children, there were six of us in the family but four were born in the United States. And in June she came in here with nowhere to go but up there, and that is the history of how they arrived into our valley.

I understand there was no mail service. There wasn't anything, and somehow or other, they— a slip-up came and she arrived in Vernon with four kids and a few trunks and what have you, practically without financial means or anything else, and no one to meet her at the old Coldstream Motel in Vernon across from the station. And as Mother many times has told me, if she could only have found some way or had the money to have got a train out and gone, she would have been gone because, understand this, Mother and Dad had never lived in the country in their life. They had always been in town. And to hit the bush, as they saw it, the year after the railroad came into Vernon and get stranded in Vernon with not knowing where Dad was or where she was going.

She had written and then, of course, as you understand, you have to pick it up with a saddle horse and take it out to Creighton Valley, and someone had mislaid the letter and it was a couple of days late when they suddenly found this letter to Mother— or to Dad, that she was arriving on

The Monashee Mountains. Photo: NA-11333/BC Forest Service

Around 1910, hockey was a serious pastime in Lumby. Photo: B-02001

that certain date. And when she arrived there was just no one there to meet her. And, of course, there was no communication or anything, so she didn't know where she sat or whether Dad was here or somewhere else. [laughs] But within a couple of days Dad arrived down in Vernon with an old wagon to pick her up. [laughs]

Pre-empt land, that's all there was in this country. Dad thought that of the future of a great agricultural valley and he pre-empted 320 acres. The old property is up there. I many times go by it and have a look at it. It has memories. I never lived there. They moved out of there. I believe that the main object was when I was born, they had to get nearer to somewhere to live. The other children had to go to school and that is when they moved down into the Lumby district. That was when I was born here. '97.

Well, Lumby as I remember my first impression, of course, was a central point here. I believe it was White Valley at that time when we first remember it and then it was called after this old chap—the government agent Lumby in Vernon—and became Lumby, but it was actually a wide spot in the road, you know. There had to be someplace for, oh, you might say a hotel to start and a post office and a little store, and that was first as I remember it. The store, I believe, was run by Louis Morand. The hotel was probably Louis Christian and my first impressions of that old Louis Christian and then after that, of course, many others have arrived that I knew— I knew all those old chaps.

So I would say that how they originated here going back into the older people— and I do know many of them because when I was just going to school here, and I did start to school here in 1904, in this village is when I first went to school. And them old-timers, many of them were still here at that time. And on top of that, they would be at our home visiting and then they would speak about the old-timers before them, so it's just like I did know. Very vividly, the old-timers talking about them, and it was yesterday, talking about them as yesterday.

They were French Canadians. This was a French Canadian settlement, and you'll find they came through— Them days, transportation, of course—water, overland—had to be where there, if there was no road it had to be the type of country you could travel overland. So they came with the missionary, French missionaries up through the Okanagan Valley and settled into Okanagan Mission. A great many of them came in there and then moved from Okanagan Mission at Kelowna, expanded out into the district here to pre-empt land, and I think the oldest ones, that's where you'll find they came through. And I know many of them like old Mr. Christian and all those. They originated through the Okanagan Mission, through the Catholic Mission at Kelowna.

Then you had the other type, like Old Man Bonnell and several others that came through from New Westminster overland with a wagon. The Cariboo Trail got them as far as Ashcroft and then after that they branched into a type of country, that rangy country that they could drive their wagons into Enderby and they arrived at the other Catholic Mission that's at the Enderby end. The priests had come out and formed a mission like the mission down here at Kelowna or at O'Keefe's and then they advertised that or brought these people out to there. And they congregated around it.

And when we were here—first in many years—there was very few of us that were not Catholics in this town. We were raised with them, and finer people you never lived with. The people that populated it, it's going away now. You don't see that anymore; we're on equal basis: even you can't pick nationalities out anymore. They've intermarried and live together, but at one time it was just different. It's hard to describe them. They were a class of people. It's hard to understand young people at 17 or 18 years old leaving Quebec with a way around, probably right down through Oregon and up the Pacific Coast to get into Lumby, and they had to be of a pioneer spirit. And then following them, the women came in here the same, and old, old families that were around, to take off into the wilderness the same as they did, 4,000 miles from home. But they were a wonderful class of people. Hard workers, very hard workers and very fine, generous-hearted people. They had to be. You lived off the land and one would help the other. That's the only way I can explain them.

They were hard workers, loggers, they came here to clear land for cattle. First this was a stock country, naturally at the start of this country that is the first thing you can do anything with was cattle, and so it was cattle, and then try to clear enough land to get feed for them and increase. When I was young, all we knew was saddle horses and cattle, and eventually other things, industry, took the place of that; we found other work and employment. But that was my first impression of here was all these chaps with their cattle, maybe a hundred head, 150 head, eventually grew up to that big. It was a cattle country.

I can remember on going to school days when they rolled logs into this creek right here in the river drive and drove them down this creek to the river and into Enderby. That's hard to believe, that you could drive logs down this creek, but I still saw them rolling logs in right off this bank here, right in front of this house. That was one of the first big things, that was the first industry in the country and the big mill was at Enderby. And so it started in by logging here on the creeks and the only transportation you had was the high water. And that's what they worked on.

We were a French Canadian town so there was numerous of them, our French Canadians, and somebody had to nickname us something, so they called us "The Flying Frenchmen." But when hockey started in here—I would say about 1909 or '10, in that bracket—Dave Hardy came in here from Nelson; he was about 16 years old. His father moved into here and Dave came in here, he was a young chap from Nelson. And he was playing hockey then at 16 years old with the two Patricks in Nelson. He was playing in between the two Patricks so you can understand he could have gone with them but his dad wouldn't let him go; he was a boy and he brought him here. But when he came in here, of course, he had

us right down on the creek here on the ice—
there used to be a dam here and the creek
was backed up so we had ice. And I can very
well remember his first winter here he had us
down there cutting sticks on the bank, you
know, he was showing us the right kind of a
crook for a hockey stick and we were playing
on the creek with Dave Hardy.

And a lot of people going through here
and I can very well remember them and
many people like Doug Barber and Bonny
and Coony Witmore, the two Conn brothers;
they were all old senior hockey players and
of a high calibre. The next year we started
hockey in this town with an open-air rink and
we started senior hockey, not intermediate or
junior. In this little town they were playing
senior hockey on the first rink; all outside fellows and wonderful hockey players.

Lester Patrick, one of the early legends of hockey,
played all over BC and helped develop the sport.
Photo courtesy of the Hockey Hall of Fame

That would be back, I would say 1910–
1910 or '11, in that bracket; somebody can contradict me along the way,
but it's around that time when we started senior hockey in this town. And
of course it followed, and hockey became quite a thing in here. And you
can understand that you'll always start hockey from the type of hockey
you're taught. And that's what created that great little town of Lumby
as a hockey town: starting from watching senior hockey players operate,
not something that they didn't know. You know, when you start from that
other bracket where you're all learning, you don't get that. But they were
watching real hockey players, and then we had the junior, intermediate and senior, we had three hockey teams in here. And of course I was
junior at that time, and it wasn't very many years until we got away from
senior hockey, the Flying Frenchmen days, and that's when I came in,
and that was not too late in years. And my old skates, the last pair I had,
are hanging up in the basement still.

We have had the provincial championship once in this town, and we

The Lumby Flying Frenchmen—a rich history of champions. Photo courtesy of the Lumby & District Historical Society.

were always a threat to anyone. No matter where they went, we were always a threat to them. And we've had some very fine hockey players. Louis Norris went to school— was brought up with me, played six years in Trail. High-score man in Trail six years, and he came from this little town when he went over there. Paddy Murphy, who was born in Vernon, played with our juniors that broke the second year, broke them in. He was signed to the New York Rangers from here and then he went to school in Spokane—he was contracted to the New York Rangers right from this little hockey town. A promising junior, that's what he was, and they had seen it.

I Can Go to My Grave a Contented Man

WARREN CROWE

on Honouring the Founder of Rossland

(RECORDED SEPTEMBER 14, 1964)

In 1890, deposits of gold-copper were found in the Monashee Mountain range. A major gold rush ensued. When Ross Thompson (1865–1951), a prospector and miner, arrived on the "least-sloping side" of Red Mountain, he found a settlement called Red Mountain Camp. The camp consisted of a collection of canvas tents over sticky, muddy ground. However, a wagon road was being built to transport ore to Butte, Montana, for smelting.

Thompson spent a year in that camp hacking away at the mountainside and then realized there was an opportunity to make a fortune as a landowner in a gold-rich location such as Red Mountain Camp. In 1892 he staked out the 160 acres where the camp was located for pre-emption. He later took on some partners, built the Clifton Hotel and started to sell lots. He renamed the town Thompson. He was later informed that there was another town in BC with that name (the other Thompson no longer exists), so he changed the name to Rossland. By the time Rossland was incorporated on March 18, 1897, there were 7,000 people living there and the town had seventeen law firms, eight doctors' offices and forty-two saloons. Thompson sold the last of his lots in 1904 and moved to Nevada. According to Warren Crowe (1895–1972), this was not the end of the story for Ross Thompson.

Warren Crowe was just 5 years old when he moved from Londonderry, Nova Scotia, to Rossland with his family in 1899. He enlisted in the

Old Glory Mountain, Rossland, ca. 1900. B-04802

army in 1916 and fought as a private with the 131st Battalion during the Great War. Crowe moved back to Rossland after the war and became a prominent member of the community. Mount Crowe, a popular skiing destination located near Rossland, was named for him.

· · ·

CD3, TRACK 11 WARREN CROWE: I was born in Londonderry in Nova Scotia in 1895. And we came to Rossland. Dad came out in 1898, and the family followed in 1899. Now, just to give a little instance in regards to my mother, her family consisted of three—and my aunt, and she had five children. So imagine in those days what those women must've endured to bring a family of eight children across Canada with transportation that's provided in those days. You can imagine, we were, I would estimate, at least five to six days on the train, and it must've been a tremendous undertaking for them. But nevertheless, we arrived in Rossland. That was in 1899. I was just 5 years old.

I can recall, that was the strike of 1901, which would put me at 7 years, then. At that time, we didn't have any labour organizations like we have today, although the men were trying to organize. They struck in 1901, and I can recall that a good many evening we went to bed with just a piece of bread, without any— We didn't have such a thing as butter; well, we couldn't afford it in the first place. And it was certainly a hardship was endured by all people. We didn't get no assistance at all from— The men stayed out on strike, and I forget the duration of that strike, I'd say about eight or nine months, possibly. But the times were getting pretty difficult, and the men finally agreed to go back to work for a little better conditions, and a little more consideration was given.

We had— those days, in the wintertime, the powder would come in, say, in carload lots, and was put into a, well, what we called a powder magazine. You'd classify it, possibly, as a warehouse. Although it was built underground, like dugouts we had in the First War. And the powder was stored in there, but the powder would become froze, and in order to use it, it had to be thawed out. Well, in this powder magazine, there was one man always detailed to look after the powder while it was being thawed out, with steam in those years. And it was during the course of the thawing out of, oh, I'd say possibly a ton, maybe a ton and a half of powder, it exploded anyway. It came in contact with something that'd detonate the powder. And at that time, with forty cases of powder, blowing up, it just took two storeys right off of the War Eagle Hotel, which was up above the bank. It just took the two storeys; it broke every window in Rossland, and shoved in doors and windows.

And us kids were sleigh-riding way down about a mile beyond Rossland, and we heard of this tremendous explosion, and we all rushed up, heading for home, of course. And when we got up near the town, this girl came out and said, "Oh, I don't know what's happened." She said, "I seen people's heads and bodies flying through the air." It wasn't so, but nevertheless it certainly scared us, and we rushed home, of course. When we did, we found home in deplorable condition, the windows all shattered out, and of course, the folks were worried about us children, but that was a major disaster. 1905 was the time the powder house, that was that incident.

And one man that does stand out was Ross Thompson. Us children going to school, we heard so much, and wrote essays on him, and everything. Well, here, some sixteen years ago [1948], I went to Vancouver, and Frank Woodside, who was then the president of the Chamber of Mines, who was a personal friend of mine, he said, "If you can be here tomorrow afternoon, Warren, there's somebody coming that you'll enjoy meeting." And I said, "Well," I said, "Who is it?" He wouldn't commit himself to who it was. He

Ross Thompson, founder of Rossland. Photo courtesy of the Rossland Museum

said, "You be here," and I said, "I certainly will." So I was there the next afternoon, this little wizard old man dropped in, kind of dried-up old fella. Frank smiled on his face, and I knew, but I couldn't recall, I couldn't visualize who the party might be. And when he stepped inside of this little enclosure where Frank and I were sitting, he says, "Now, Warren, I want you to meet Ross Thompson." Well, I just felt something from within that— meeting a man that I've heard so much about, and read so much about. So after enjoying his company for, oh, some three or four hours, I suggested (Mrs. Crowe was down there with us), I suggested he come out for dinner with us in the evening, which he declined, and declined very sharply, which I couldn't reason within what was driving— what I'd said, probably. But the way he refused the offer, I thought, "Well, it must be something that I've said, or something that I've done that maybe has offended him." So, I told him, I said, "Well, could I meet you tomorrow afternoon?" He says, "Yes," he said, "It would be a pleasure." So I kind of felt a little better.

And, nevertheless, I got down there early next morning and went to Frank and said, "Frank, what did I do to Ross yesterday?" I said, "I extended him an invitation to come out and have dinner with... We were going to any place that he would've named." I said, "We're just down here on a visit..." I said, "His refusal was so sharp," I said, "it kind of got under my hide." Well, he said, "Don't you know the reason?" I said, "No, I don't, Frank. What is it?" Well, he said, "He can't retaliate," and he said, "He hates to accept anything." Well, I said, "That was farthest from my thought." But I said, "Now that you have put it," I said, "I suppose I'm not welcome, but," I said, "I'd like to be able to help him out." He said, "Don't do that," he said, "you might offend him." So I met him the next day and enjoyed his company. But I come back to Rossland with one intention in mind, to have that old fellow up as our guest.

I went to several organizations and different— I put the suggestion forth; it wasn't highly entertained. So, finally I thought, "Well, to heck with you all." I just took three days off and I went— or, I made up a list and I went— I'm going to start this right now. I went right up after Billy Esling, who was the Member of Parliament. I said, "Billy, I'm undertaking to do something that I feel there's justification for." And I said, "I'm going to ask you to head a list. I'm asking for a donation." He said, "I know of no better gesture," he said, "I think this is just wonderful." He said, "Any suggestions?" I said, "No, it's up to you, but don't forget there's going to be lots to follow, so don't go to any extreme." Billy was quite able to go to any figure if he wanted to. "Well," he said, "how do you suppose $50?" I said that'd be fine. I went from him right up to Lorne Campbell, who was quite a— well, he was an old-timer, and he was married to the West Kootenay Power. And I went around with my list and put my cards

When Ross Thompson discovered there was already a city named Thompson in BC, he imaginatively named his new community Rossland. Photo: D-04249

on the table. Well, everybody was really in accordance with being able to donate to a fund of that kind. So I went ahead and I raised quite a few hundred dollars. And I just went to the bank and put it into Ross Thompson's account, and got a chequebook and a passbook, and made arrangements: sent Frank Woodside $100 and told him to get a hold of— and have the old fellow to come up to be our guest for a couple of months.

I didn't say anything to anybody, just got the car when the day came and I went out to Castlegar and met him, and brought him into Trail. When we got halfway in, he just stood there and looked, and he said, "Goodness, isn't it good to be able to travel by automobile where I walked," he said, "to record to my homestead in Rossland?" I just dug in my pocket, I said, "Here, Ross, here's a little something that's been raised by the local people in Rossland, by the business people, and we hope you enjoy your visit there." So I just turned it right over to him.

And Ross came up here, and I went to Mr. Diamond, when they had a banquet, and I said, "Now if you people want to do something, put on a banquet." I said, "Now, Mr. Diamond, you've been very fair throughout this," and I said, "there's one favour I'd like to ask further of you." "Well, Mr. Diamond," I said, "He'd walked all through. He still has some

Rossland in the 1890s. Photo: B-06825

friends." I said, "Johnny Harris in Sandon, some people in Kaslo and some people in Nelson whom he would like to see." And I said, "We have modern conveyance. If you could see your way possible to provide transportation for him." I said, "I know it'd be appreciated by him and the rest of us, too." He said, "That's a small request," he said. "Your wish will be granted." So I went and told Ross, I said, "They're planning a little trip for you." I said, "Where you can visit Johnny Harris in Sandon, where you can go to Kaslo and visit your friends, where you can go to Nelson, where you walked through this country." I said, "We've got modern means, and you're going out." Well, he just thought that was fine.

So the date was arranged. He was staying at the Allan Hotel. This big car drove up, a brand new car with a driver, with a full bottle of Scotch right alongside of the driver. That was for his personal use. So they drove him to Sandon. He spent one day in Sandon with Johnny Harris, and I guess talked about the old times, and went to Kaslo and met some more of his friends. He was gone four days on the trip. The full cost of that trip was born by CMNS [today known as Teck Metals], and every morning he got up there was a brand new bottle of Scotch there, which the old fellow liked very much. Well, during the course of his visit up here, I did, I kept little articles that would appear in the press, I made a little scrapbook. Well, when Ross comes down, he says, "I don't know how to thank the people of Rossland," he said, "I've enjoyed this," he said, "I can go to my grave a contented man." It'd given me a lot of satisfaction.

And he went back to Vancouver, and Woodside told me, you know, he's just like a 2-year-old kid. He was running around the streets, rambled— showing the people this book, you know. And the old fellow didn't last very long after that. In a few months, the old fellow had died, but I think most people were glad of the opportunity to be able to afford him those, which he was fully entitled to.

Acknowledgements

A PROJECT of this scope requires the contributions of many people and organizations. I am very thankful to the following:

Imbert Orchard and Ian Stephen for deciding to be the two renegades of the CBC, travelling all over British Columbia in the first half of the 1960s. Their hard work, dedication and vision led them to all corners of the province, by all means of transportation, to interview 998 "old-timers," which has given British Columbians the gift of one of the largest oral history collections in the world! The collection in this book, as well as the one in *Voices of British Columbia*, comprises a small sample of their hard work.

There are several people at the CBC who have been tremendous supporters of my work. First off, immense gratitude to Sheryl MacKay for allowing me the opportunity to bring forth this amazing collection as a regular part of her show, *North by Northwest*. I am also very thankful to Mark Forsythe, Jo-Ann Roberts, Deborah Wilson, Kirstie Hudson and Gregor Craigie for the amazing and important work they do on and off the air.

Colin Preston of the CBC Archives in Vancouver for working so hard in preserving the colourful history the CBC has captured for future generations to learn from and enjoy. Moreover, he has granted permission for the audio to be used in this book.

Gary Mitchell of the Royal BC Museum and BC Archives for donating all the photos in this book (except those noted). The partnership between the museum and the CBC is the underlying collaboration that made this three-dimensional experience of BC's history possible. I know Orchard would be thrilled!

All of the curators, preservationists and archivists (past and present) at the BC Archives who have worked so hard to maintain the history of our province. There are too many to mention, but they include Dennis Duffy, Allen Specht, J. Robert Davison, David Lemieux, Derek Swallow, Cheryl Linstead, Ember Lundgren, Kelly-Ann Turkington, Derek Reimer, Charlene Gregg, Martina Steffen, Kathryn Bridge, Michael Carter, Claire Gilbert, Katy Hughes, Ann ten Cate and all the reference room staff, among many others.

I had to do a ton of research to put together the background information for each story in this book. To aid in my study, I relied on the exceptional scholarship of John Lutz, Robin Fisher and Jean Barman for reference. I would also like to thank Dave Obee, Amy Smart and Georgie Hay for their help with some hard-to-find photos.

Furthermore, I reached out and contacted family members of several interviewees, all of whom were more than happy to help in this endeavour. Their contributions helped bring many of these stories to life. Special heartfelt thanks to Nick Orchard; Shelley Stephen; the Orchard and Stephen families; Nita, Herb and Amelia Morven; Heather Maclaren, Marian Hargrove and Gail Hotell.

My mentors, colleagues, and supporters in the University of Victoria History department. These include Eric Sager, Karen Hickton, Wendy Wickwire, Georgia Sitara, Greg Blue, John Lutz, Rick Rajala, Tom Saunders and Elizabeth Vibert.

Special thanks to Sam Sullivan and Jay Powell for sharing their rich expertise of Chinook Wawa.

I also wish to thank my editor Lucy Kenward, who enthusiastically poured her energy into this project. Also to Anna Comfort O'Keeffe, Howard White, Shed Simas, Annie Boyar, Zoe Grams and the rest of the tremendous team at Harbour. I can't express how fortunate I am that they support and encourage my vision on this and many other undertakings.

The audio recordings included in this book are very true to the original masters made by Ian Stephen on those reel-to-reels all those years ago. Special thanks to Chris Van Sickle and Marc Jenkins for their help with the fine tuning to make these discs sound just exactly perfect.

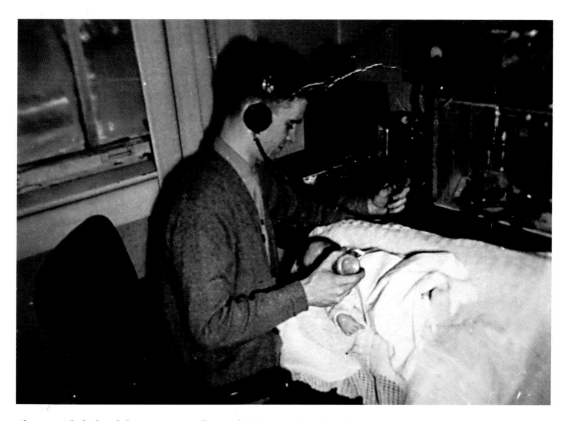

Always with the headphones on: recording technician Ian Stephen takes inspiration
from an older generation while tending to the needs of a generation yet to come.
Photo courtesy of Amy Stephen